The colonizer
and
the colonized

The colonizer and the colonized

Albert Memmi

EXPANDED EDITION

Introduction by Jean-Paul Sartre
Afterword by Susan Gilson Miller

Beacon Press   Boston

Beacon Press
Boston, Massachusetts
www.beacon.org

Beacon Press books
are published under the auspices of
the Unitarian Universalist Association of Congregations.

21 20 19 18   23

This book is printed on acid-free paper that meets the uncoated paper
ANSI/NISO specifications for permanence as revised in 1992.

Library of Congress Cataloging-in-Publication Data
Memmi, Albert.
    [Portrait du colonisé, précédé du portrait du colonisateur. English]
    The colonizer and the colonized / by Albert Memmi ;
introduction by Jean-Paul Sartre ; afterword by Susan Gilson Miller ;
[translated by Howard Greenfeld].—Expanded ed.
        p.   cm.
    Translation of: Portrait du colonisé précédé du portrait du colonisateur.
    Reprint, with new afterword. Originally published: 1st American ed.
New York : Orion Press, 1965.
    ISBN 978-0-8070-0301-5 (pbk.)
    1. Colonies. 2. Indigenous peoples.   I. Title.
JV51.M413   1991
325'.3—dc20   90-24035
                                                               CIP

The American edition
is dedicated to
the American Negro,
also colonized,
and to
Howard Greenfeld,
my publisher
and friend

Preface

1965

It would be untrue to say that I foresaw the full significance of this book in 1957 when I wrote it. I had written a first novel, *The Pillar of Salt,* a life story which was in a sense a trial balloon to help me find the direction of my own life. However, it became clear to me that a real life for a cultured man was impossible in North Africa at that time. I then tried to find another solution, this time through the problems of a mixed marriage, but this second novel, *Strangers,* also led me nowhere. My hopes then rested on the "couple," which still seems to me the most solid happiness of man and perhaps the only real answer to solitude. But I discovered that the couple is not an isolated entity, a forgotten oasis of light in the middle of the world; on the contrary, the whole world is within the couple. For my unfortunate protagonists, the world was that of colonization. I felt that to understand the failure of their undertaking, that of a mixed marriage in a colony, I first had to understand the colonizer and the colonized, perhaps the entire colonial relationship and situation. All this was leading me far from myself and from my own problems, but their explanation became more and more complex; so without knowing where I would end up, I had to at least try to put an end to my own anguish.

It would be equally untrue to say that my ambition in painting this portrait of one of the major oppressions of our time was to describe oppressed peoples in general; it was not even my intention to write about all colonized people. I was Tunisian, therefore colonized. I discovered that few aspects of my life and my personality were untouched by this fact. Not only my own thoughts, my passions and my conduct, but also the conduct of others towards me was affected. As a young student arriving at the Sorbonne for the first time, certain rumors disturbed me. As a Tunisian, would I be allowed to sit for the examinations in philosophy? I went to see the president of the jury. "It is not a right," he explained. "It is a hope." He hesitated, a lawyer looking for the exact words. "Let us say that it is a colonial hope." I have yet to understand what that meant in fact, but I was unable to get anything more out of him. It can be imagined with what serenity I worked after that.

Thus, I undertook this inventory of conditions of colonized people mainly in order to understand myself and to identify my place in the society of other men. It was my readers—not all of them Tunisian— who later convinced me that this portrait was equally theirs. My travels and conversations, meetings and books convinced me, as I advanced in my work on the book, that what I was describing was the fate of a vast multitude across the world. As I discovered that all colonized people have much in common, I was led to the conclusion that all the oppressed are alike in some ways. Nonetheless, while I was writing this book, I preferred to ignore these conclusions that today I maintain are undeniable. So many different persons saw themselves in this portrait that it became impossible to pretend that it was mine alone, or only that of colonized Tunisians, or even North Africans. I was told that in many parts of the world the colonial police confiscated the book in the cells of militant nationalists. I am convinced that I gave them nothing they did not already know, had not already experienced; but as they recognized their own emotions, their revolt, their aspirations, I suppose they appeared more legitimate to them. Above all, whatever the truthfulness of this description of our common experience, it struck them less than the coherence of ideas which I put forward. When the Algerian war was about to break out, I predicted first to myself and then to others the probable dynamism of events. The colonial relationship which I had tried to define chained the colonizer and the colonized into an implacable dependence, molded their respective characters and dictated their conduct. Just as there was an obvious logic in the reciprocal behavior of the two colonial partners, another mechanism, proceeding from the first, would lead, I believed, inexorably to the decomposition of this dependence. Events in

Algeria confirmed my hypothesis; I have often veri-
fied it since then in the explosion of other colonial
situations.

The sum of events through which I had lived since
childhood, often incoherent and contradictory on the
surface, began to fall into dynamic patterns. How
could the colonizer look after his workers while
periodically gunning down a crowd of the colonized?
How could the colonized deny himself so cruelly yet
make such excessive demands? How could he hate
the colonizers and yet admire them so passionately?
(I too felt this admiration in spite of myself.) I
needed to put some sort of order into the chaos of
my feelings and to form a basis for my future actions. By temperament and education I had to do this
in a disciplined manner, following the consequences
as far as possible. If I had not gone all the way, trying to find coherence in all these diverse facts, recon-
structing them into portraits which were answerable
to one another, I could not have convinced myself
and would have remained dissatisfied with my effort.
I saw, then, what help to fighting men the simple,
ordered description of their misery and humiliation
could be. I saw how explosive the objective revela-
tion to the colonized and the colonizer of an essentially explosive condition could be. It was as if the
unveiling of the fatality of their respective paths
made the struggle the more necessary and the delay-

ing action the more desperate. Thus, the book escaped from my control.

I must admit I was a bit frightened of it myself. It was clear that the book would be utilized by well-defined colonized people—Algerians, Moroccans, African Negroes. But other peoples, subjugated in other ways—certain South Americans, Japanese and American Negroes—interpreted and used the book. The most recent to find a similarity to their own form of alienation have been the French Canadians. I looked with astonishment on all this, much as a father, with a mixture of pride and apprehension, watches his son achieve a scandalous and applauded fame. Nor was all this uproar totally beneficial, for certain parts of the book of great importance to me were obscured—such as my analysis of what I call the Nero complex; and that of the failure of the European left in general and the Communist Party in particular, for having underestimated the national aspect of colonial liberation; and, above all, the importance, the richness, of personal experience. For I continue to think, in spite of everything, that the importance of this endeavor is its modesty and initial particularity. Nothing in the text is invented or supposed or even hazardously transposed. Actual experience, co-ordinated and stylized, lies behind every sentence. If in the end I have consented to a general tone, it is because I know that I could, at every line, every word, produce innumerable concrete facts.

I have been criticized for not having constructed my portraits entirely around an economic structure, but I feel I have repeated often enough that the idea of privilege is at the heart of the colonial relationship—and that privilege is undoubtedly economic. Let me take this opportunity to reaffirm my position: for me the economic aspect of colonialism is fundamental. The book itself opens with a denunciation of the so-called moral or cultural mission of colonization and shows that the profit motive in it is basic. I have often noted that the *deprivations* of the colonized are the almost direct result of the advantages secured to the colonizer. However, colonial privilege is not solely economic. To observe the life of the colonizer and the colonized is to discover rapidly that the daily humiliation of the colonized, his objective subjugation, are not merely economic. Even the poorest colonizer thought himself to be—and actually was—superior to the colonized. This too was part of colonial privilege. The Marxist discovery of the importance of the economy in all oppressive relationships is not to the point. This relationship has other characteristics which I believe I have discovered in the colonial relationship. But, one might ask, in the *final analysis,* don't these phenomena have a more or less hidden economic aspect? Isn't the motivating force of colonization economic? The answer is maybe —not certainly. We don't actually know what man is, or just what is essential to him; whether it is money or sex or pride. . . . Does psychoanalysis win out over Marxism? Does all depend on the individual or on society? In any case, before attacking this *final analysis* I wanted to show all the real complexities in the lives of the colonizer and the colonized. Psychoanalysis or Marxism must not, under the pretext of having discovered the source or one of the main sources of human conduct, pre-empt all experience, all feeling, all suffering, all the byways of human behavior, and call them profit motive or Oedipus complex.

I put forward another example which will probably go against my cause; but I believe that as a writer I must state everything, even that which can be used against me. My portrait of the colonized, which is very much my own, is preceded by a portrait of the colonizer. How could I have permitted myself, with all my concern about personal experience, to draw a portrait of the adversary? Here is a confession I have never made before: I know the colonizer from the inside almost as well as I know the colonized. But I must explain: I said that I was a Tunisian national. Like all other Tunisians I was treated as a second-class citizen, deprived of political rights, refused admission to most civil service departments, etc. But I was not a Moslem. In a country where so many groups, each jealous of its own physiognomy, lived side by side, this was of considerable importance. The Jewish population identified as much with the colonizers as with the colonized. They were undeniably "natives," as they were then called, as near as possible to the Moslems in poverty, language, sensibilities, customs, taste in music, odors and cooking. However, unlike the Moslems, they passionately endeavored to identify themselves with the French. To them the West was the paragon of all civilization, all culture. The Jew turned his back happily on the East. He chose the French language, dressed in the Italian style and joyfully adopted every idiosyncrasy of the Europeans. (This, by the way, is what all colonized try to do before they pass on to the stage of revolt.) For better or for worse, the Jew found himself one small notch above the Moslem on the pyramid which is the basis of all colonial societies. His privileges were laughable, but they were enough to make him proud and to make him hope that he was not part of the mass of Moslems which constituted the base of the pyramid. It was enough to make him feel endangered when the structure began to crumble. The Jews bore arms side by side with the French in the streets of Algiers. My own relations with my fellow Jews were not made any easier when I decided to join the colonized, but it was necessary for me to denounce colonialism, even though it was not as hard on the Jews as it was on the others. Because of this ambivalence I knew only too well the contradictory emotions which swayed their lives.

Didn't my own heart beat faster at the sight of the little flag on the stern of the ships that joined Tunis to Marseille?

All this explains why the portrait of the colonizer was in part my own—projected in a geometric sense. My model for the portrait of the colonizer of good will was taken in particular from a group of philosophy professors in Tunis. Their generosity was unquestionable; so, unfortunately, was their impotence, their inability to make themselves heard by anyone else in the colony. However, it was among these men that I felt most at ease. While I was virtuously busy debunking the myths of colonization, could I complacently approve of the counter-myths fabricated by the colonized? I could but smile with my friends at their halting assurance that Andalusian music is the most beautiful in the world; or that Europeans are fundamentally bad (the proof being that they are too harsh with their children). Naturally the result was suspicion on the part of the colonized. And this in spite of the immense good will of this type of French colonizer and the fact that these Frenchmen were already despised by the rest of the French community. I understood only too well their difficulties, their inevitable ambiguity and the resulting isolation; more serious still, their inability to act. All this was a part of my own fate.

Shall I go even further? Though I could not approve of them, I understood even the hard-core colonizers (*pieds noirs*)—they were more simple in thought and action. As I have stated repeatedly, a man is a product of his objective situation; thus I had to ask myself if I would have condemned colonization so vigorously if I had actually benefited from it myself. I hope so, but to have suffered from it only slightly less than the others did has made me more understanding. The most blindly stubborn *pied noir* was, in effect, my born brother. Life has treated us differently; he was the legitimate son of France, heir to privileges which he would defend at any price whatsoever; I was a sort of half-breed of colonization, understanding everyone because I belonged completely to no one.

This book has caused as much anguish and anger as it has enthusiasm. On the one hand, people saw it as an insolent provocation; on the other, a flag to which to rally. Everyone agreed on its militant aspect. It seemed to be an arm in the war against colonization, and indeed it has become one. But nothing seems more ridiculous to me than to boast of borrowed courage and feats never accomplished. I have mentioned how relatively naïve I was when I wrote this book. Then I simply wanted to understand the colonial relationship to which I was bound. I am not saying that my philosophy was alien to my search, my anger and, in a way, my whole life. I am unconditionally opposed to all forms of oppression. For me, oppression is the greatest calamity of humanity. It diverts and pollutes the best energies of man—of oppressed and oppressor alike. For if colonization destroys the colonized, it also rots the colonizer. Be that as it may, provocation was not the object of my work. The effectiveness of the material came gratuitously by the sole virtue of truth.

It was probably sufficient to describe with precision the facts of colonization, the manner in which the colonizer was bound to act, the slow and inevitable destruction of the colonized, to bring to light the absolute iniquity of colonization; and, at the same time, to unveil the fundamental instability of it and predict its demise. My only merit was to have endeavored, over and above my own uneasiness, to describe an unbearable, therefore unacceptable, aspect of reality, one which was destined to provoke continuing upheavals, costly for everyone. Instead of reading this book for its scandalous content or as a permanent provocation to revolt, I hope the reader will calmly examine why these conclusions were reached, conclusions which continue to be reached spontaneously by so many people in similar situations. Is this not simply because these two portraits are faithful to their models? They don't have to recognize themselves in my mirror to discover all by themselves the most useful course of action in their lives of misery. Everyone knows the confusion which still exists between the artist and his subject. Instead of being irritated by what writers say, and accusing them of trying to create disturbances which they only describe and announce, it would be better to listen more attentively and take their warnings more seriously. Do I not have the right, after so many disastrous and useless colonial wars, to think that this book could have been useful to the colonizer as well as to the colonized?

A.M.
PARIS, 1965

Contents

Introduction

Only the Southerner is competent to discuss slavery, because he alone knows the Negro; the puritanical and abstract Northerners know man only as an entity. This fine line of reasoning still has its uses: in Houston, in the newspapers of New Orleans, and in "French" Algeria—since we too are someone's Northerners. The newspapers there tell us that the colonizer alone is qualified to speak of the colony. The rest of us, who live in the mother country, do not have his experience, so we are to view the burning land of Africa through his eyes, which will just show us the smoke.

For those intimidated by this criminal line of reasoning, I recommend the reading of *The Colonizer and the Colonized*. Here, experience is matched against experience. The author, a Tunisian, told of his bitter youth in *The Pillar of Salt*. Exactly who is he? Colonizer or colonized? He would say "neither"; you, perhaps, would say "both"—it amounts to the same thing. He belongs to one of those native but non-Moslem groups that are "more or less privileged in comparison with the colonized masses, but . . . rejected . . . by the colonizing group," which, however, "does not completely discourage" their efforts to integrate themselves into European society. Linked by actual liabilities to the subproletariat, but separated from it by meager privileges, the members of this group live in a constant state of uneasiness. Memmi himself has experienced a twofold liability, a twofold rejection, in the process that sets colonizers against colonized, and "self-rejecting colonizers" against "self-accepting colonizers." He has understood the system so well because he felt it first as his own contradiction. He explains very clearly in the book that such rendings of the spirit, plainly introjections of social conflicts, do not dispose the individual to action. But the man who suffers them, if he becomes aware of himself, can enlighten others through his self-examination: a "negligible force in the confrontation," he *represents* no one, but since he *is* everyone at once, he will prove to be the best of witnesses.

But Memmi's book is not a chronicle. The author may feed on memories, but he has assimilated them all. The book is rather the *formulation* of an experience: caught between the racist usurpation of the colonizers and the building of a future nation by the colonized, where the author "suspects he will have no place," he attempts to live his particularity by transcending it in the direction of the universal. The transcendence is not toward Man, who does not yet exist, but toward a rigorous reason enforcing its claims on everyone. This lucid and sober work may be classed among the "passionate geometries," for its calm objectivity represents transcendence of suffering and anger.

This is doubtless the reason Memmi might be reproached for his seeming idealism; in fact, he tells all. But one can haggle with him about his method. Perhaps it would have been better to show the colonizer and his victim both throttled by the colonial *apparatus*, that cumbersome machine, constructed at the close of the Second Empire and under the Third Republic, that now, after giving the colonizers every satisfaction, turns against them and threatens to crush them. In fact, racism is built into the system: the colony sells produce and raw materials cheaply, and purchases manufactured goods at very high prices from the mother country. This singular trade is profitable to both parties only if the native works for little or nothing. The colonial agricultural subproletariat cannot even count on an alliance with the least-favored Europeans, for everyone lives off them, even the "small colonizers," whom the big proprietors exploit, but who are privileged compared to the Algerians, the average income of the Algerian Frenchman being ten times that of the Algerian Moslem. Here the tension is born. To keep salaries and the cost of living at a minimum, there must be great competition among native workers, so the birth rate must rise; but since the country's resources are earmarked for colonialist appropriation, the Moslem standard of living, on constant wages, continues to fall. The population thus lives in a chronic state of malnutrition. Conquest occurred through violence, and over-exploitation and oppression necessitate continued violence, so the army is present. There would be no contradiction in that, if terror reigned everywhere in the world, but the colonizer enjoys, in the mother country, democratic rights that the colonialist system refuses to the colonized native. In fact, the colonialist system favors population growth to reduce the cost of labor, and it forbids assimilation of the natives, whose numerical superiority, if they had voting rights, would shatter the system. Colonialism denies human rights to human beings whom it has subdued by violence, and keeps them by force in a state of misery and ignorance that Marx would rightly call a subhuman condition. Racism is ingrained in actions, institutions, and in the nature of the colonialist methods of production and exchange. Political and social regulations reinforce one another. Since the native is subhuman, the Declaration of Human Rights does not apply to him; inversely, since he has no rights, he is abandoned without protection to inhuman forces—brought in with the colonialist praxis, engendered every moment by the colonialist apparatus, and sustained by relations of production that define two sorts of individuals—one for whom privilege and humanity are one, who becomes a human being through exercising his rights; and the other, for whom a denial of rights sanctions misery, chronic hunger, ignorance, or, in general, "subhumanity." I have always thought that ideas take form from things and that the ideas are already within man when he awakens them and expresses them to elucidate his situation. The colonizer's "conservatism" and "racism," his ambiguous relations with the mother country—such things are given *first*, before he revives them into Nero complexes.

Memmi would no doubt reply that he is saying nothing else. I know that. (Does he not say, "The colonial situation manufactures colonizers as it manufactures colonies?" The whole difference between us arises perhaps because he sees a situation where I see a system.) Moreover, perhaps it is Memmi who is right in expressing his ideas in the order of discovery; that is, starting with human intentions and felt relationships, he guarantees the genuineness of his experience. He suffered first in his relations with others and in his relations with himself; he encountered the objective structure in thoroughly studying the contradiction that was rending him, and he delivers structure and contradiction up to us just as they are, raw and still permeated with his subjectivity.

Let us stop haggling. The work establishes some strong truths. First of all, that there are neither good nor bad colonists: there are colonialists. Among these, some reject their objective reality. Borne along by the colonialist apparatus, they do every day in reality what they condemn in fantasy, for all their actions contribute to the maintenance of oppression. They will change nothing and will serve no one, but will succeed only in finding moral comfort in malaise.

The others—by far the greater number—sooner or later accept themselves.

Memmi has strikingly described the sequence of steps that leads them to "self-absolution." Conservatism brings about the selection of mediocre men. How can an elite of usurpers, aware of their mediocrity, establish their privileges? By one means only: debasing the colonized to exalt themselves, denying the title of humanity to the natives, and defining them as simply absences of qualities—animals, not humans. This does not prove hard to do, for the system deprives them of everything. Colonialist practice has engraved the colonialist idea into things themselves; it is the movement of things that designates colonizer and colonized alike. Thus oppression justifies itself through oppression: the oppressors produce and maintain by force the evils that render the oppressed, in their eyes, more and more like what they would have to be like to deserve their fate. The colonizer can only exonerate himself in the systematic pursuit of the "dehumanization" of the colonized by identifying himself a little more each day with the colonialist apparatus. Terror and exploitation dehumanize, and the exploiter authorizes himself with that dehumanization to carry his exploitation

further. The engine of colonialism turns in a circle;
it is impossible to distinguish between its praxis and
objective necessity. Moments of colonialism, they
sometimes condition one another and sometimes
blend. Oppression means, first of all, the oppressor's
hatred for the oppressed. There exists a solitary limit
to this venture of destructiveness, and that is colonialism itself. Here the colonizer encounters a contradiction of his own: "Were the colonized to disappear, so would colonization—with the colonizer."
There would be no more subproletariat, no more
over-exploitation. The usual forms of capitalistic exploitation would reassert themselves, and prices and
wages would fall into line with those of the mother
country. This would spell ruin. The system wills
simultaneously the death and the multiplication of
its victims. Any transformation would be fatal to the
system. Whether the colonized are assimilated or
massacred, the cost of labor will rise. The onerous
engine suspends between life and death, and always
closer to death, those who are compelled to drive it.
A petrified ideology devotes itself to regarding human beings as talking beasts. But it does so in vain,
for the colonizers must recognize them first, even to
give them the harshest or most insulting of orders.
And since the colonizers cannot constantly supervise
the colonized, the colonizers must resolve to trust
them. No one can treat a man like a dog without first
regarding him as a man. The impossible dehumaniza-

tion of the oppressed, on the other side of the coin, becomes the alienation of the oppressor. It is the oppressor himself who restores, with his slightest gesture, the humanity he seeks to destroy; and, since he denies humanity in others, he regards it everywhere as his enemy. To handle this, the colonizer must assume the opaque rigidity and imperviousness of stone. In short, he must dehumanize himself, as well.

A relentless reciprocity binds the colonizer to the colonized—his product and his fate. Memmi has vividly recorded this. With him, we find that the colonialist system is a form in motion, born towards the middle of the last century, that will manufacture its own destruction of itself. For a long time now, colonialism has cost mother countries more than it has earned. France is crushed under the burden of Algeria, and we now know that we shall abandon the war, without victory or defeat, when we are too poor to pay for it. It is above all the rigidity of the colonialist apparatus that is causing its breakdown. The old social structures are pulverized, the natives are "atomized"—and colonialist society cannot integrate them without destroying itself. Thus the colonized must rediscover their unity in opposition to that society. The excluded human beings will affirm their exclusivity in national selfhood. Colonialism creates the patriotism of the colonized. Kept at the level of a beast by an oppressive system, the natives are given no rights, not even the right to live. Their condition worsens daily. And when a people has no choice but how it will die; when a people has received from its oppressors only the gift of despair, what does it have to lose? A people's misfortune will become its courage; it will make, of its endless rejection by colonialism, the absolute rejection of colonization. The secret of the proletariat, Marx once said, is that it bears within it the destruction of bourgeois society. We must be grateful to Memmi for reminding us that the colonized likewise has his secret, and that we are witnessing the infamous death-struggle of colonialism.

Jean-Paul Sartre
PARIS, 1957

Translated by Lawrence Hoey

PART ONE

PORTRAIT OF THE COLONIZER

Does
the colonial
exist?

We sometimes enjoy picturing the colonizer as a tall man, bronzed by the sun, wearing Wellington boots, proudly leaning on a shovel—as he rivets his gaze far away on the horizon of his land. When not engaged in battles against nature, we think of him laboring selflessly for mankind, attending the sick, and spreading culture to the nonliterate. In other words, his pose is one of a noble adventurer, a righteous pioneer.

I don't know whether this portrait ever did correspond to reality or whether it was limited to the engravings on colonial bank notes. Today, the economic motives of colonial undertakings are revealed by every historian of colonialism. The cultural and moral mission of a colonizer, even in the beginning, is no longer tenable.

Today, leaving for a colony is not a choice sought because of its uncertain dangers, nor is it a desire of one tempted by adventure. It is simply a voyage towards an easier life. One need only ask a European living in the colonies what general reasons induced him to expatriate and what particular forces made him persist in his exile. He may mention adventure, the picturesque surroundings or the change of environment. Why then, does he usually seek them where his own language is spoken, where he does not find a large group of his fellow countrymen, an administration to serve him, an army to protect him? The adventure would have been less predictable; but that sort of change, while more definite and of better quality, would have been of doubtful profit. The change involved in moving to a colony, if one can call it a change, must first of all bring a substantial profit. Spontaneously, better than language scholars, our traveler will come up with the best possible definition of a colony: a place where one earns more and spends less. You go to a colony because jobs are guaranteed, wages high, careers more rapid and business more profitable. The young graduate is offered a position, the public servant a higher rank, the businessman substantially lower taxes, the industrialist raw materials and labor at attractive prices.

However, let us suppose that there is a naïve person who lands just by chance, as though he were going to Toulouse or Colmar. Would it take him long to discover the advantages of his new situation? The economic meaning of a colonial venture, even if it is realized after arrival, thrusts itself upon us no less strongly, and quickly. Of course, a European in the colonies can also be fond of this new land and delight in its local color. But if he were repelled by its climate, ill at ease in the midst of its strangely dressed crowds, lonely for his native country, the problem would be whether or not to accept these nuisances and this discomfort in exchange for the advantages of a colony.

Soon he hides it no longer; he is often heard dreaming aloud: a few more years and he will take leave of this profitable purgatory and will buy a house in his own country. From then on, even though fed up, sick of the exotic, at times ill, he hangs on; he will be trapped into retirement or perhaps death. How can he return to his homeland if this would mean cutting his standard of living in half? Go back to the viscous slowness of progress at home?

It is this simple reasoning which delays their return, even though life has become difficult, if not dangerous, during the recent past. Even those who are called birds of passage in the colony do not show too much haste to leave. An unexpected fear of disorientation arises as soon as they begin to plan the return home. Realizing that they have been away from their country long enough to have no more living acquaintances, we can understand them in part. Their children were born in the colony and it is there that their dead are buried. But they exaggerate their anguish. In organizing their daily habits in the colonial community, they imported and imposed the way of life of their own country, where they regularly spend their vacations, from which they draw their administrative, political and cultural inspiration, and on which their eyes are constantly fixed.

Their change of environment is really one of economics: that of a *nouveau riche* taking a chance on becoming poor.

They will therefore carry on as long as possible, for the more time passes, the longer the advantages last, and these advantages are, after all, worth a little concern. But if one day his livelihood is affected, if "situations" are in real danger, the settler then feels threatened and, seriously this time, thinks of returning to his own land.

The matter is even clearer on a collective plane. Colonial ventures have never had any other avowed meaning. During the French-Tunisian negotiations, a few naïve persons were astonished by the relative good will shown by the French government, particularly in the cultural field, then by the prompt acquiescence of the leaders of the colony. The reason is that the intelligent members of the bourgeoisie and colony had understood that the essence of colonization was not the prestige of the flag, nor cultural expansion, nor even governmental supervision and the preservation of a staff of government employees. They were pleased that concessions could be made in all areas if the basis (in other words, if the economic advantages) were preserved. And if M. Mendès-France was able to make his famous lightning trip, it was with their blessing and under the protection of one of their own. That was exactly his program and the primary content of the agreements.

Having found profit either by choice or by chance,

the colonizer has nevertheless not yet become aware of the historic role which will be his. He is lacking one step in understanding his new status; he must also understand the origin and significance of this profit. Actually, this is not long in coming. For how long could he fail to see the misery of the colonized and the relation of that misery to his own comfort? He realizes that this easy profit is so great only because it is wrested from others. In short, he finds two things in one: he discovers the existence of the colonizer as he discovers his own privilege.

He knew, of course, that the colony was not peopled exclusively by colonists or colonizers. He even had some idea of the colonized from his childhood books; he had seen a documentary movie on some of their customs, preferably chosen to show their peculiarity. But the fact remained that those men belonged to the realms of imagination, books or the theater. His concern with them came indirectly—through images which were common to his entire nation, through military epics or vague strategic considerations. He had been a little worried about them when he too had decided to move to a colony, but no more so than he was about the climate, which might be unfavorable, or the water, which was said to contain too much limestone. Suddenly these men were no longer a simple component of geographical or historical décor. They assumed a place in his life.

He cannot even resolve to avoid them. He must

constantly live in relation to them, for it is this very alliance which enables him to lead the life which he decided to look for in the colonies; it is this relationship which is lucrative, which creates privilege. He finds himself on one side of a scale, the other side of which bears the colonized man. If his living standards are high, it is because those of the colonized are low; if he can benefit from plentiful and undemanding labor and servants, it is because the colonized can be exploited at will and are not protected by the laws of the colony; if he can easily obtain administrative positions, it is because they are reserved for him and the colonized are excluded from them; the more freely he breathes, the more the colonized are choked. While he cannot help discovering this, there is no danger that official speeches might change his mind, for those speeches are drafted by him or his cousin or his friend. The laws establishing his exorbitant rights and the obligations of the colonized are conceived by him. As for orders which barely veil discrimination, or apportionment after competitive examinations and in hiring, he is necessarily in on the secret of their application, for he is in charge of them. If he preferred to be blind and deaf to the operation of the whole machinery, it would suffice for him to reap the benefits; he is then the beneficiary of the entire enterprise.

It is impossible for him not to be aware of the constant illegitimacy of his status. It is, moreover,

in a way, a double illegitimacy. A foreigner, having
come to a land by the accidents of history, he has
succeeded not merely in creating a place for himself
but also in taking away that of the inhabitant, granting himself astounding privileges to the detriment
of those rightfully entitled to them. And this not by
virtue of local laws, which in a certain way legitimize
this inequality by tradition, but by upsetting the established rules and substituting his own. He thus
appears doubly unjust. He is a privileged being and
an illegitimately privileged one; that is, a usurper.
Furthermore, this is so, not only in the eyes of the
colonized, but in his own as well. If he occasionally
objects that the privileged also exist among the
bourgeois colonized, whose affluence equals or ex-
ceeds his, he does so without conviction. Not to be
the only one guilty can be reassuring, but it cannot
absolve. He would readily admit that the privileges
of privileged natives are less scandalous than his. He
knows also that the most favored colonized will
never be anything but colonized people, in other
words, that certain rights will forever be refused
them, and that certain advantages are reserved
strictly for him. In short, he knows, in his own eyes
as well as those of his victim, that he is a usurper.
He must adjust to both being regarded as such, and
to this situation.

Before seeing how these three discoveries—profit,
privilege, and usurpation, these three developments

of the colonizer's conscience—will shape his appearance, by what mechanisms they will transform the colonial candidate into a colonizer or colonialist, we must answer a frequent objection. It is often said that a colony does not contain only colonists. Can one talk of privileges with respect to railroad workers, minor civil servants or even small farmers, who will probably live as well as their counterparts back home?

To agree on a convenient terminology, let us distinguish among a colonial, a colonizer and the colonialist. A colonial is a European living in a colony but having no privileges, whose living conditions are not higher than those of a colonized person of equivalent economic and social status. By temperament or ethical conviction, a colonial is a benevolent European who does not have the colonizer's attitude toward the colonized. All right! Let us say right away, despite the apparently drastic nature of the statement: a colonial so defined does not exist, for all Europeans in the colonies are privileged.

Naturally, not all Europeans in the colonies are potentates or possess thousands of acres or run the government. Many of them are victims of the masters of colonization, exploited by these masters in order to protect interests which do not often coincide with their own. In addition, social relationships are almost never balanced. Contrary to everything which we like to think, the small colonizer is actually, in most cases, a supporter of colonialists and an obstinate defender of colonial privileges. Why?

Solidarity of fellow man with fellow man? A defensive reaction, an expression of anxiety by a minority living in the midst of a hostile majority? Partly. But during the peak of the colonial process, protected by the police, the army, and an air force always ready to step in, Europeans in the colonies were not sufficiently afraid to explain such unanimity. It is certain that they were not just-minded. It is true that the small colonizer himself would have a fight to carry on, a liberation to bring about; if he were not so seriously fooled by his own naïveté and blinded by history. But I do not believe that gullibility can rest on a complete illusion or can completely govern human conduct. If the small colonizer defends the colonial system so vigorously, it is because he benefits from it to some extent. His gullibility lies in the fact that to protect his very limited interests, he protects other infinitely more important ones, of which he is, incidentally, the victim. But, though dupe and victim, he also gets his share.

However, privilege is something relative. To different degrees every colonizer is privileged, at least comparatively so, ultimately to the detriment of the colonized. If the privileges of the masters of colonization are striking, the lesser privileges of the small colonizer, even the smallest, are very numerous. Every act of his daily life places him in a relationship with the colonized, and with each act his fundamental advantage is demonstrated. If he is in trouble with the law, the police and even justice will be more lenient toward him. If he needs assistance from the government, it will not be difficult; red tape will be cut; a window will be reserved for him where there is a shorter line so he will have a shorter wait. Does he need a job? Must he take an examination for it? Jobs and positions will be reserved for him in advance; the tests will be given in his language, causing disqualifying difficulties for the colonized. Can he be so blind or so blinded that he can never see that, given equal material circumstances, economic class or capabilities, he always receives preferred treatment? How could he help looking back from time to time to see all the colonized, sometimes former schoolmates or colleagues, whom he has so greatly outpaced?

Lastly, should he ask for or have need of anything, he need only show his face to be prejudged favorably by those in the colony who count. He enjoys the preference and respect of the colonized themselves, who grant him more than those who are the best of their own people; who, for example, have more faith in his word than in that of their own population. From the time of his birth, he possesses a qualification independent of his personal merits or his actual class. He is part of the group of colonizers whose values are sovereign. The colony follows the cadence of his traditional holidays, even religious holidays, and not those of the inhabitants. The weekly day of rest is that of his native country; it is his nation's flag which flies over the monuments, his mother tongue which permits social communication. Even his dress, his accent and his manners are eventually imitated by the colonized. The colonizer partakes of an elevated world from which he automatically reaps the privileges.

It is also their concrete economic and psychological position within the colonial society in relation to the colonized on one hand, and to the colonizers on the other hand, which accounts for the traits of the other human groups—those who are neither colonizers nor colonized. Among these are the nationals of other powers (Italians, Maltese of Tunisia), candidates for assimilation (the majority of Jews), the recently assimilated (Corsicans in Tunisia, Spaniards in Algeria). To these can be added the representatives of the authorities recruited among the colonized themselves.

The poverty of the Italians or Maltese is such that it may seem ludicrous to speak of privileges in connection with them. Nonetheless, if they are often in want, the small crumbs which are automatically accorded them contribute toward differentiating them —substantially separating them from the colonized. To whatever extent favored as compared to the colonized masses, they tend to establish relationships of the colonizer-colonized nature. At the same time, not corresponding to the colonizing group, not having the same role as theirs in colonial society, they each stand out in their own way.

All these nuances are easily understandable in an analysis of their relationship with colonial life. If the Italians in Tunisia have always envied the French for their legal and administrative privileges, they are nevertheless in a better situation than the colonized. They are protected by international laws and an extremely watchful consulate under constant observation by an attentive mother country. Often, far from being rejected by the colonizer, it is they who hesitate between integration and loyalty to their homeland. Moreover, the same European origin, a common religion and a majority of identical customs bring them sentimentally closer to the colonizer. The results are definite advantages which the colonized certainly does not have: better job opportunities; less insecurity against total misery and illness; less precarious schooling; and a certain esteem on the part of the colonizer accompanied by an almost respectable dignity. It will be understood that, as much as they may be outcasts in an absolute sense, their behavior vis-à-vis the colonized has much in common with that of the colonizer.

On the other hand, benefiting from colonization by proxy only, the Italians are much less removed from the colonized people than are the French. They do not have that stilted, formal relationship with them, that tone which always smacks of a master addressing his slave, which the French cannot entirely shed. In contrast to the French, almost all the Italians speak the language of the colonized, make long-lasting friendships with them and even—a particularly revealing sign—mixed marriages. To sum up, having no special reason to do so, Italians do not maintain a great distance between themselves and the colonized. The same analysis would apply, subject to some minor differences, to the Maltese.

The situation of the Jewish population—eternally hesitant candidates refusing assimilation—can be viewed in a similar light. Their constant and very justifiable ambition is to escape from their colonized condition, an additional burden in an already oppressive status. To that end, they endeavor to resemble the colonizer in the frank hope that he may cease to consider them different from him. Hence their efforts to forget the past, to change collective habits, and their enthusiastic adoption of Western language, culture and customs. But if the colonizer does not always openly discourage these candidates to develop that resemblance, he never permits them to attain it either. Thus, they live in painful and constant ambiguity. Rejected by the colonizer, they share in part the physical conditions of the colonized and have a communion of interests with him; on the other hand, they reject the values of the colonized as belonging to a decayed world from which they eventually hope to escape.

The recently assimilated place themselves in a considerably superior position to the average colonizer. They push a colonial mentality to excess, display proud disdain for the colonized and continually show off their borrowed rank, which often belies a vulgar brutality and avidity. Still too impressed by their privileges, they savor them and defend them with fear and harshness; and when colonization is imperilled, they provide it with its most dynamic defenders, its shock troops, and sometimes its instigators.

The representatives of the authorities, cadres, policemen, etc., recruited from among the colonized, form a category of the colonized which attempts to escape from its political and social condition. But in so doing, by choosing to place themselves in the colonizer's service to protect his interests exclusively, they end up by adopting his ideology, even with regard to their own values and their own lives.

Having been fooled to the point of accepting the inequities of his position, even at times profiting from this unjust system, the colonized still finds his situation more of a burden than anything else. Their contempt may be only a compensation for their misery, just as European anti-Semitism is so often a

convenient outlet for misery. Such is the history of
the pyramid of petty tyrants: each one, being socially
oppressed by one more powerful than he, always
finds a less powerful one on whom to lean, and becomes a tyrant in his turn. What revenge and what
pride for a noncolonized small-time carpenter to
walk side by side with an Arab laborer carrying a
board and a few nails on his head! All have at least
this profound satisfaction of being negatively better
than the colonized: they are never completely en-
gulfed in the abasement into which colonialism
drives them.

The colonial does not exist, because it is not up to
the European in the colonies to remain a colonial,
even if he had so intended. Whether he expressly
wishes it or not, he is received as a privileged person
by the institutions, customs and people. From the
time he lands or is born, he finds himself in a factual
position which is common to all Europeans living in
a colony, a position which turns him into a colonizer.
But it is not really at this level that the fundamental
ethical problem of the colonizer exists; the problem
of involvement of his freedom and thus of his responsibility. He could not, of course, have sought a
colonial experience, but as soon as the venture is be-
gun, it is not up to him to refuse its conditions. If he
was born in the colonies of parents who are colonizers themselves, or if, at the time of his decision, he

really was not aware of the true meaning of colonization, he could find himself subject to those conditions, independent of any previous choice.

The fundamental questions are directed to the colonizer on another level. Once he has discovered the import of colonization and is conscious of his own position (that of the colonized and their necessary relationship), is he going to accept them? Will he agree to be a privileged man, and to underscore the distress of the colonized? Will he be a usurper and affirm the oppression and injustice to the true inhabitant of the colony? Will he accept being a colonizer under the growing habit of privilege and illegitimacy, under the constant gaze of the usurped? Will he adjust to this position and his inevitable self-censure?

The colonizer
who refuses

If every colonial immediately assumes the role of colonizer, every colonizer does not necessarily become a colonialist. However, the facts of colonial life are not simply ideas, but the general effect of actual conditions. To refuse means either withdrawing physically from those conditions or remaining to fight and change them.

It sometimes happens that a new arrival—astonished by the large number of beggars, the children wandering about half-naked, trachoma, etc., ill at ease before such obvious organization of injustice, revolted by the cynicism of his own fellow citizens ("Pay no attention to poverty! You'll see: you soon get used to it!"), immediately thinks of going home. Being compelled to wait until the end of his contract, he is liable to get used to the poverty and the rest. But it may happen that this man, whose only wish was to be a colonial, finds himself unfit for this role, and soon leaves.

It can also happen that he does not leave. Having discovered the economic, political and moral scandal of colonization, he can no longer agree to become what his fellow citizens have become; he decides to remain, vowing not to accept colonization.

Oh, this vow is not necessarily a rigid one! Such

indignation is not always accompanied by desire for a policy of action. It is rather a position of principle. He may openly protest, or sign a petition, or join a group which is not automatically hostile toward the colonized. This already suffices for him to recognize that he has simply changed difficulties and discomfort. It is not easy to escape mentally from a concrete situation, to refuse its ideology while continuing to live with its actual relationships. From now on, he lives his life under the sign of a contradiction which looms at every step, depriving him of all coherence and all tranquillity.

What he is actually renouncing is part of himself, and what he slowly becomes as soon as he accepts a life in a colony. He participates in and benefits from those privileges which he half-heartedly denounces. Does he receive less favorable treatment than his fellow citizens? Doesn't he enjoy the same facilities for travel? How could he help figuring, unconsciously, that he can afford a car, a refrigerator, perhaps a house? How can he go about freeing himself of this halo of prestige which crowns him and at which he would like to take offense?

Should he happen to rationalize this contradiction so as to come to terms with this discomfort, his fellow citizens would take it upon themselves to awaken him. First with ironical indulgence; they have known, they understand this somewhat naïve uneasiness of the new arrival; it will leave him as a result of the tests of colonial life, under a multitude of small and pleasant compromises.

It *must* leave him, they insist, for humanitarian romanticism is looked upon in the colonies as a serious illness, the worst of all dangers. It is no more or less than going over to the side of the enemy.

If he persists, he will learn that he is launching into an undeclared conflict with his own people which will always remain alive, unless he returns to the colonialist fold or is defeated. Wonder has been expressed at the vehemence of colonizers against any among them who put colonization in jeopardy. It is clear that such a colonizer is nothing but a traitor. He challenges their very existence and endangers the very homeland which they represent in the colony. However, historical relationships are on their side. What would logically result from the attitude of a colonizer who rejects colonization? Why shouldn't they vigorously defend themselves against an attitude which would end in their immolation, perhaps on the altar of justice, but, nevertheless, in their sacrifice? If they only fully recognized the injustice of their position! But it is they themselves who accepted it and who made the most of it. If this newly arrived colonizer cannot rise above this intolerable moralism which prevents him from living, if he believes in it so fervently, then let him begin by going away. He will give proof of the earnestness of his feelings and will solve his problems—and stop creating them for his fellow citizens. Otherwise, he must not expect to continue to harass them undisturbed. They will take the offensive and return blow for blow. His friends will become surly; his superiors will threaten him; even his wife will join in and cry—a woman is less concerned about humanity in an abstract sense, the colonized mean nothing to her and she only feels at home among Europeans.

Is there then no way out except submission to the heart of the colonial community or departure? Yes, still one. Since his rebellion has closed the doors of colonization to him and isolated him in the middle of the colonial desert, why not knock at the door of the colonized whom he defends and who would surely open their arms to him in gratitude? He has discovered that one of the camps is that of injustice; the other, then, is that of righteousness. Let him take one more step, let him complete his revolt to the full. The colony is not made up only of Europeans! Refusing the colonizers, damned by them: let him adopt the colonized people and be adopted by them; let him become a turncoat.

There are so few of those colonizers, even of extreme good will, who seriously consider following this path, that the actual problem is rather theoretical; but it is a problem of significance in terms of an accurate view of colonial life. To refuse colonization is one thing; to adopt the colonized and be adopted by them seems to be another; and the two are far from being connected.

To succeed in this second conversion, our man would have to be a moral hero. We said he should have broken economically and administratively with the oppressors' camp. That would be the only way to silence them. What a decisive demonstration, to abandon a fourth of his income or disregard the favors of the administration! But let us drop this; it is certainly admitted today that one can be, while awaiting the revolution, both a revolutionary and an exploiter. He discovers that if the colonized have justice on their side, if he can go so far as to give them his approval and even his assistance, his solidarity stops here; he is not one of them and has no desire to be one. He vaguely foresees the day of their liberation and the reconquest of their rights, but does not seriously plan to share their existence, even if they are freed.

A trace of racism? Perhaps, without being too well aware of it. Who can completely rid himself of bigotry in a country where everyone is tainted by it, including its victims? Is it so natural to assume, even mentally, the burden of a fate on which weighs such heavy scorn? How would he, in any case, go about attracting himself to this scorn which sticks to the person of the colonized? And how could he visualize sharing in any future liberation, being himself already free? All this is really nothing but mental exercise.

Well no, it is not necessarily racism. He has simply had the time to realize that a colony is not an extension of the home country and that he is not on his home grounds. That is not inconsistent with his positions of principle. Since he has discovered the colonized and their existential character, since the colonized have suddenly become living and suffering humanity, the colonizer refuses to participate in their suppression and decides to come to their assistance. At the same time, he has understood that he has only changed his province; he has another civilization before him, customs differing from his own, men whose reactions often surprise him, with whom he does not feel deep affinity.

He will certainly have to admit this—even if he refuses to acknowledge it to the colonialists. He cannot help judging those people and that civilization. How can one deny that they are under-developed, that their customs are oddly changeable and their culture outdated? Oh, he hastens to reply, those defects are not attributable to the colonized but to decades of colonization which galvanized their history. Some colonialist arguments disturb him at times. For example, before colonization, weren't the colonized already backward? If they let themselves be colonized, it is precisely because they did not have the capacity to fight, either militarily or technically. Understanding that, their past shortcomings mean nothing as far as their future is concerned. No one doubts that they would make up for that, if they had their freedom back. He has complete faith in the genius of people, all peoples. The fact remains, however, that he admits to a fundamental difference between the colonized and himself. Colonial actuality is a specific historical fact; the situation and state of the colonized, as they presently are, of course, are none the less special.

The little strains of daily life will support him in his decisive discovery more than great intellectual convulsions will. Having first eaten *couscous* with curiosity, he now tastes it from time to time out of politeness and finds that "it's filling, it's degrading and it's not nourishing." It is "torture by suffocation," he says humorously. Or if he does like *couscous,* he cannot stand that "fairground music" which seizes and deafens him each time he passes a café. "Why so loud? How can they hear each other?" He is tortured by that odor of old mutton fat which stinks up many of the houses. Many traits of the colonized shock or irritate him. He is unable to conceal the revulsions he feels and which manifest themselves in remarks which strangely recall those of a colonialist. It was really a long time ago that he was certain, *a priori,* of the identity of human nature in every dimension. True, he still believes in it, but rather like an abstract universality or an ideal to be found in history of the future.

You are going too far, someone will remark; your benevolent colonizer is no longer so benevolent. He has evolved slowly and is he not already a colonialist? Not at all! One simply cannot live, especially for a lifetime, in what remains something picturesque and to an extent removed from one's natural sphere. As a tourist one can become enamored and perhaps interested in it for a time, but one ends up tiring of it and shielding himself from the original attraction. To live without anguish, one must live in detachment from oneself and the world—one must reconstruct the odors and sounds of one's childhood. It is not difficult to do this as it only requires spontaneous actions and mental attitudes. It would be as absurd to demand that the colonizer be attuned to the life of the colonized, as it would be to ask left-wing intellectuals to ape laborers. These intellectuals, having insisted on dressing sloppily, wearing shirts for days on end, and walking in hobnailed shoes, soon realized the stupidity of their pose, and in this case the language, cuisine and basic customs were the same. Unlike the intellectual, however, the colonizer can only reject being identified in any way with the colonized.

"Why not wear a tarboosh in Arab countries and

dye your face black in Negro countries?" an irritated teacher once asked me.

It is not immaterial to add that that teacher was a communist.

That much said, I am quite willing to admit that excessive romanticizing of the difference must be avoided. It may be thought that the benevolent colonizer's difficulties in adapting are not very important. The essential factor is firmness of ideological attitude and condemnation of colonization. (On the condition, obviously, that those difficulties do not end up in obstructing the rectitude of ethical judgment.) To be a rightist or leftist is not merely a way of thinking but also—perhaps especially—a way of feeling and of living. Let us just note that there are very few colonizers who do not allow themselves to be overcome by those revulsions and those doubts, and furthermore, these nuances must be taken into consideration in order to understand their relationship with the colonized and colonial life.

Suppose then that our benevolent colonizer has succeeded in laying aside both the problem of his own privileges and that of his emotional difficulties. Only his ideological and political attitudes remain to be considered.

A communist or socialist or just a democrat, he remained so in the colony. He intended, no matter what changes might occur in his own individual or national feeling, to continue to be one; or better still, to act like a communist, socialist or democrat. In other words, he would work toward economic equality and social liberty, expressed in the colony by a struggle for liberation of the colonized and equality between colonizers and colonized.

Here we deal with one of the most curious chapters of the history of the contemporary left (if one had dared write it) and which might be entitled "Nationalism and the Left."

In the face of nationalism, an undeniable uneasiness exists in the European left. Socialism has already tried for so long to have an internationalist bent that this tradition has seemed to be tied to its doctrine and to form part of its fundamental principles. With leftists of my generation, the word "nationalist" still evokes a reaction of suspicion, if not hostility. When the U.S.S.R., the "international fatherland" of socialism, established itself as a nation, the reasons for doing so did not appear convincing to many of its most devoted admirers. We remember that recently, the governments of the peoples threatened by Nazism resorted to somewhat forgotten national responses. This time, the workers' parties, awakened by the Russian example, discovered that national pride remained powerful among their troops and responded to that call. The French Communist Party even took it up for its own use and laid claim to being a "national party," reinstating the Tricolor and the *Marseillaise*. And it was again that tactic—or that revival—which prevailed after the war against the investment in those old nations by young America. Rather than fight as socialists against a capitalist danger, the communist parties (and a large part of the left) preferred to put one national entity in opposition to another; in the process, confusing Americans with capitalists. The result was a decided constraint in the socialist attitude toward nationalism (an irresolution in the ideology of the workers' parties). The caution employed by left-wing journalists and essayists who commented on this problem is extremely revealing. They deal with as little as possible; they don't dare to condemn or approve; they don't know how to, or whether they want to integrate it, to include it in their understanding of the historical future. In a word, the left today feels ill at ease before nationalism.

For a number of historical, sociological and psychological reasons, the struggle for liberation by colonized peoples has taken on a marked national and nationalistic look. While the European left cannot but approve, encourage, and support that struggle, it suffers from very intense doubts and real uneasiness in the face of the nationalistic form of those attempts at liberation. In addition, the nationalistic renaissance of the workers' parties is above all a form for the same socialist content. Everything happens as though social liberation, which remains the ultimate goal, were embodied in more or less permanent national form; the Internationals had simply buried nations too soon. But the leftist does not always clearly understand the immediate social content of the struggle of nationalistic colonized peoples. In short, the leftist finds in the struggle of the colonized, which he supports *a priori,* neither the traditional means nor the final aims of that left wing to which he belongs. And it follows that this uneasiness is distinctly aggravated in a left-wing colonizer, i.e., a leftist living in a colony and living his daily life within that nationalism.

Take terrorism, one example among the methods used in that struggle. We know that leftist tradition condemns terrorism and political assassination. When the colonized uses them, the leftist colonizer becomes unbearably embarrassed. He makes an effort to separate them from the colonized's voluntary action; to make an epiphenomenon out of his struggle. They are spontaneous outbursts of masses too long oppressed, or better yet, acts by unstable, untrustworthy elements which the leader of the movement has difficulty in controlling. Even in Europe, very few people admitted that the oppression of the colonized was so great, the disproportion of forces so overwhelming, that they had reached the point, whether morally correct or not, of using violent means voluntarily. The leftist colonizer tried in vain to explain actions which seemed incomprehensible, shocking and politically absurd. For example, the death of children and persons outside of the struggle, or even of colonized persons who, without being basically opposed, disapproved of some small aspect of the undertaking. At first he was so disconcerted that the best he could do was to deny such actions; for they would fit nowhere in his view of the problem. That it could be the cruelty of oppression which explained the blind fury of the reaction hardly seemed to be an argument to him; he can't approve acts of the colonized which he condemns in the colonizers because these are exactly why he condemns colonization.

Then, after having suspected the information to be false, he says, as a last resort, that such deeds are errors, that is, that they should not belong to the essence of the movement. He bravely asserts that the leaders certainly disapprove of them. A newspaperman who always supported the cause of the colonized, weary of waiting for censure which was not forthcoming, finally called on certain leaders to take a public stand against the outrages. Of course, he received no reply; he did not have the additional naïveté to insist.

Confronted with this silence, what was there to do? He tried to interpret the phenomenon for himself and for the sake of his uneasiness to explain it to others, but never, it must be said, to justify it. The leaders cannot and will not speak though they are aware of this terrorism. He would have accepted with relief, with joy, the slightest indication of understanding. And since these indications cannot come, he finds himself in an unenviable dilemma: either likening the colonial situation to any other and therefore applying to it the same analytical methods, judging it and the colonized in accordance with traditional values; or he must consider the colonial juncture as being original and abandon his values and usual habits of political thought which induced him to take sides. In other words, either he no longer recognizes the colonized, or he no longer recognizes himself. However, being unable to bring himself to select one of these paths, he stays at the crossroads and loses contact with reality. He applies to one and to the other those ulterior motives which he deems convenient and portrays a colonized according to his reconstruction. In short, he begins to construct myths.

He is also worried about the future of the liberation of the colonized, at least about its near future. Often the liberated nation asserts itself beyond the limits of the struggle, and aspires, for example, to be religious, or shows no concern for individual freedom. Again there is no way out except to assume a hidden, bolder, and nobler motive. In their hearts, all the lucid and responsible fighters are anything but theocrats; they really love and venerate freedom. It is the immediate crisis which causes them to disguise their true feelings; faith still being strong among the colonized masses, they must take it into account. As for their apparent disregard for democracy, it can be explained by the fact that since they need the support of all groups, they are afraid to alienate the powerful bourgeois and land-owning classes.

But terrorism does not coincide with the leftist colonizer's stride toward liberation and his uneasiness remains deep-rooted, often reappearing. The leaders of the colonized cannot criticize the religious feelings of their troops—that the left-wing colonizer will admit—but to exploit them is another thing! Those proclamations in the name of God, the Holy War concept, for instance, throws the leftist off balance and frightens him. Is it purely strategic? How can he fail to notice that when freed, the most newly liberated nations hasten to include religion in their constitutions, or that their laws conform to the premises of liberty and democracy which the leftist colonizer expected?

Then, fearing that he might be wrong once again, he will retreat; he will speculate on a more distant future. Later, assuredly, leaders will arise from the midst of those peoples who will express their honest needs, who will defend their true interests, in harmony with the moral (and socialist) imperatives of history. It was inevitable that only the bourgeoisie and landowners, who had some education, would establish the framework and place their imprint on the movement. Later on, the colonized will rid themselves of xenophobia and racist temptation, which the leftist colonizer perceives, not without concern. An inevitable reaction to racism and the colonizer's xenophobia is that it becomes necessary to wait for the disappearance of colonization and the wounds which it has left in the flesh of the colonized. Later they will shake off religious obscurantism. . . .

But in the meantime, the leftist colonizer cannot help remaining confused about the meaning of the immediate battle. For him, being on the left means not only accepting and assisting the national liberation of the peoples, but also includes political democracy and freedom, economic democracy and justice, rejection of racist xenophobia and universality, material and spiritual progress. Because such aspirations mean all those things, every true leftist must support the national aspirations of people. If the leftist colonizer rejects colonization refusing his role as colonizer, it is in the name of this ideal. But now he discovers that there is no connection between the liberation of the colonized and the application of a left-wing program. And that, in fact, he is perhaps aiding the birth of a social order in which there is no room for a leftist as such, at least in the near future.

It can even happen that for various reasons—to gain the friendship of reactionary powers, to carry out a national union or out of conviction—the liberation movements banish forthwith leftist ideology and refuse systematically its assistance, thus placing it in intolerable embarrassment, condemning it to sterility. Then, as a militant left-winger, the colonizer even finds himself almost out of the movement of colonial liberation.

These very difficulties, moreover, this hesitation which curiously resembles remorse, excludes him all the more. They leave him suspect not only in the eyes of the colonized, but also in those of the left wing at home; it is from this that he suffers most. He voluntarily cut himself off from the Europeans of the colony; he disregards their insults and is even proud of them. But the leftists are truly his own people, the judges whom he appoints, before whom he desires to justify his life in the colony. Now his peers and his judges hardly understand him; the least of his timid reservations draw only distrust and indignation. What! they tell him, a people is waiting, suffering from hunger, illness and contempt, one child in four dies before he is one year old, and he wants assurances on means and ends! What conditions he sets for his co-operation! After all, this matter is one of ethics and ideology. The only task at the moment is that of freeing the people. As for the future, there will be plenty of time to deal with it when it becomes the present. Yet, he insists, the shape of post-liberation is already apparent. They will silence him with a decisive argument—in that it is simply a refusal to look that future in the face—by telling him that the destiny of the colonized does not concern him and that what the colonized will do with their freedom concerns them only.

If he wants to help the colonized, it is exactly because their destiny does concern him, because his destiny and theirs are intertwined and matter to one another, because he hopes to go on living in the colony. He cannot help thinking bitterly that the attitude of the leftists back home is really an abstract one. Granted, at the time of the resistance against the Nazis, the only task which was imperative and which united all the fighters was liberation. But all of them fought for a certain political future as well. If the left-wing groups, for example, had been assured that the future regime would be theocratic and authoritarian, or the rightist groups that it would be communist, if they had realized that for imperative sociological reasons they would be crushed after the battle, would they both have gone on fighting? Perhaps. But would their hesitations or their fears have seemed so offensive? Believing that socialism was exportable and Marxism universal, the leftist colonizer wonders whether he has not failed through excessive pride. In this matter, he believed he had the right to fight for his conception of the world in accordance with the one in which he hoped to build his life.

The left at home, as well as the colonized themselves, agree that he should withdraw (and on top of this, curiously, the colonialist, which confirms the heterogeneity of mentalities). He will support the colonized's unconditional liberation, by whatever means they use, and the future which they seem to have chosen for themselves. A journalist of the best French left-wing weekly ended up admitting that man's fate could mean achieving the Koran and supporting the Arab League. The Koran, all right; but the Arab League! Must the just cause of a people include its deceptions and errors? The leftist colonizer will accept all the ideological themes of the struggling colonized; he will temporarily forget that he is a leftist.

To succeed in becoming a turncoat, as he has finally resolved to do, it is not enough to accept the position of the colonized, it is necessary to be loved by them.

The first point was not reached without difficulties or serious contradictions because he had to abandon his basic political values. The intellectual or the progressive bourgeois might want the barriers between himself and the colonized to fade; those are class characteristics which he would gladly renounce. But no one seriously aspires toward changing language, customs, religious affiliation, etc., even to ease his conscience, nor even for his material security.

The second point is no easier. In order truly to become a part of the colonial struggle, even all his good will is not sufficient; there must still be the possibility of adoption by the colonized. However, he suspects that he will have no place in the future nation. This will be the last discovery, the most staggering one for the left-wing colonizer, the one which he often makes on the eve of the liberation, though it was really predictable from the very beginning.

To understand this point, it is necessary to keep in mind an essential feature of the nature of colonial life; the colonial situation is based on the relationship between one group of people and another. The leftist colonizer is part of the oppressing group and will be forced to share its destiny, as he shared its good fortune. If his own kind, the colonizers, should one day be chased out of the colony, the colonized would probably not make any exception for him. If he could continue to live in the midst of the colonized, as a tolerated foreigner, he would tolerate together with the former colonizers the rancor of a people once bullied by them. If the home country's power should, on the other hand, endure in the colony, he would continue to harvest his share of hatred despite his manifestations of good will. To tell the truth, the style of a colonization does not depend upon one or a few generous or clear-thinking individuals. Colonial relations do not stem from individual good will or actions; they exist before his arrival or his birth, and whether he accepts or rejects them matters little. It is they, on the contrary which, like any institution, determine *a priori* his place and that of the colonized and, in the final analysis, their true relationship. No matter how he may reassure himself, "I have always been this way or that with the colonized," he suspects, even if he is in no way guilty as an individual, that he shares a collective responsibility by the fact of membership in a national oppressor group. Being oppressed as a group, the colonized must necessarily adopt a national and ethnic form of liberation from which he cannot but be excluded.

How could he help thinking, once again, that this fight is not his own? Why should he struggle for a social order in which he understands that there would be no place for him?

Hard-pressed, the role of the left-wing colonizer collapses. There are, I believe, impossible historical situations and this is one of them. The present life of the leftist colonizer in the colony is ultimately unacceptable by virtue of his ideology, and if that ideology should triumph it would question his very existence. The strict consequence of this realization would be the abandonment of that role.

He can, of course, attempt to come to terms with the situation, and his life will be a long series of adjustments. The colonized in the midst of whom he lives are not his people and never will be. After careful consideration, he cannot be identified with them and they cannot accept him. "I feel more at home with colonialist Europeans," confessed a left-wing colonizer, "than with any of the colonized." He does not foresee, if he ever did, such an assimilation; in any event, he lacks the necessary imagination for a revolution of that kind. While he happens to dream of a tomorrow, a brand-new social state in which the colonized cease to be colonized, he certainly does not conceive, on the other hand, of a deep transformation of his own situation and of his own personality. In that new, more harmonious state, he will go on being what he is, with his language intact and his cultural traditions dominating. Through a *de facto* contradiction which he either does not see in himself or refuses to see, he hopes to continue being a European by divine right in a country which would no longer be Europe's chattel; but this time by the divine right of love and renewed confidence. He would no longer be protected and ruled by his army but by the fraternity of peoples. Juridically, there would be very few minor administrative changes, the practical nature and consequences of which he cannot guess. Without having a clear legal picture, he vaguely hopes to be a part of the future young nation, but he firmly reserves the right to remain a citizen of his native country. Finally he realizes that everything may change. He invokes the end of colonization, but refuses to conceive that this revolution can result in the overthrow of his situation and himself. For it is too much to ask one's imagination to visualize one's own end, even if it be in order to be reborn another;

especially if, like the colonizer, one can hardly evaluate such a rebirth.

One now understands a dangerously deceptive trait of the leftist colonizer, his political ineffectiveness. It results from the nature of his position in the colony. His demands, compared to those of the colonized, or even those of a right-wing colonizer, are not solid. Besides, has one ever seen a serious political demand—one which is not a delusion or fantasy —which does not rest upon concrete solid supports, whether it be the masses or power, money or force? The right-wing colonizer is consistent when he demands a colonial status quo, or even when he cynically asks for more privileges and more rights. He defends his interests and his way of life, and can utilize enormous forces to support his demands. The hopes and desires of the colonized are just as clear. They are founded on latent forces which poorly realize their own power, but are capable of astonishing developments. The left-wing colonizer refuses to become a part of his group of fellow citizens. At the same time it is impossible for him to identify his future with that of the colonized. Politically, who is he? Is he not an expression of himself, of a negligible force in the varied conflicts within colonialism?

His political desires will suffer from a flaw inherent in his own anomalous position. If he attempts to begin a political group, he will interest only those who are already leftist colonizers, or other misplaced heretics. He will never succeed in attracting large numbers of the colonized or the colonizers because he threatens their interests. In a situation like this, a party of great popular expression should be derived from or directed toward them, and the leftist faction is not. He cannot try to start a strike. He would immediately discover that he is an outsider and, therefore, totally impotent. Should he agree to offer his unconditional help, that would not assure him of having any voice in events; not only that, but this air of gratuity only serves better to emphasize his political powerlessness.

The distance between his commitment and that of the colonized will have unforeseen and insurmountable consequences. Despite his attempts to take part in the politics of the colony, he will be constantly out of step in his language and in his actions. He might hesitate or reject a demand of the colonized, the significance of which he will not immediately grasp. This lack of perception will seem to confirm his indifference. Wanting to vie with the less realistic nationalists, he might indulge in an extreme type of demagogy which will increase the distrust of the colonized. When explaining the acts of the colonizer, he will offer obscure or Machiavellian rationalizations where the simple mechanics of colonization are self-explanatory. Or, to the irritated astonishment of the colonized, he will loudly excuse what the latter condemn in himself. Thus, while refusing the sinister, the benevolent colonizer can never attain the good, for his only choice is not between good and evil, but between evil and uneasiness.

In the end, the leftist colonizer cannot fail to question the success of his efforts. His fits of verbal furor merely arouse the hatred of his fellow citizens and leave the colonized indifferent. His statements and promises have no influence on the life of the colonized because he is not in power. Nor can he converse with the colonized, asking questions or asking for assurances. He is a member of the oppressors and the moment he makes a dubious gesture or forgets to show the slightest diplomatic reserve (and he believes he can permit himself the frankness authorized by benevolence), he draws suspicion. He also admits that he must not embarrass the struggling colonized by doubts and public interrogations. In short, everything confirms his solitude, bewilderment and ineffectiveness. He will slowly realize that the only thing for him to do is to remain silent. Is it necessary to say that this silence is probably not such a terrible anguish to him? That he was rather forcing himself to fight in the name of theoretical justice for interests which are not his own; often even incompatible with his own?

If he cannot stand this silence and make his life a perpetual compromise, he can end up by leaving the colony and its privileges. And if his political ethics will not permit him to "run out," he will make a fuss. He will criticize the authorities until he is "delivered to the disposal of the *metropole*," as the chaste administrative jargon goes. By ceasing to be a colonizer, he will put an end to his contradiction and uneasiness.

The colonizer
who accepts

A colonizer who rejects colonialism does not find a solution for his anguish in revolt. If he does not eliminate himself as a colonizer, he resigns himself to a position of ambiguity. If he spurns that extreme measure, he contributes to the establishment and confirmation of the colonial relationship. It is understandable that it is more convenient to accept colonization and to travel the whole length of the road leading from colonial to colonialist.

A colonialist is, after all, only a colonizer who agrees to be a colonizer. By making his position explicit, he seeks to legitimize colonization. This is a more logical attitude, materially more coherent than the tormented dance of the colonizer who refuses and continues to live in a colony. The colonizer who accepts his role tries in vain to adjust his life to his ideology. The colonizer who refuses, tries in vain to adjust his ideology to his life, thereby unifying and justifying his conduct. On the whole, to be a colonialist is the natural vocation of a colonizer.

It is customary to contrast an immigrant and a colonialist by birth. An immigrant would adopt the colonialist doctrine more slowly, while the transformation of a native colonizer into a colonialist is more inevitable. Family influence, vested interests, acquired situations, in which he lives and by which he is greatly influenced, and of which colonialism is the ideology, restrain his freedom. I do not believe, however, that the distinction is a fundamental one. The material condition of a privileged person/usurper is identical for the one who inherits it at birth and the one who enjoys it from the time he lands. A realization of what he is and of what he will become necessarily ensues, in varying degrees, if that condition is accepted.

It is a bad sign to decide to spend life in the colonies, just as it is a negative indication to marry a dowry. The immigrant who is prepared to accept anything, having come for the express purpose of enjoying colonial benefits, will become a colonialist by vocation.

The model is very ordinary and his portrait flows readily from the top of a pen. The man is generally young, prudent, and polished. His backbone is tough, his teeth long. No matter what happens he justifies everything—the system and the officials in it. He obstinately pretends to have seen nothing of poverty and injustice which are right under his nose; he is interested only in creating a position for himself, in obtaining his share. One protector sends him, another welcomes him, and his job is already waiting for him. If it should happen that he was not exactly summoned to the colony, he is soon chosen to go there. It takes little time for the colonizer's solidarity to come into play. "Can we leave a fellow citizen in difficulty?" I have seen many immigrants who, having recently arrived, timid and modest, suddenly provided with a wonderful title, see their obscurity illuminated by a prestige which surprises even them. Then, supported by the corset of their special role, they lift up their heads, and soon they assume such inordinate self-confidence that it makes them dizzy. Why should they not congratulate themselves for having come to the colony? Should they not be convinced of the excellence of the system which makes them what they are? Henceforth they will defend it aggressively; they will end up believing it to be right. In other words, the immigrant has been transformed into a colonialist.

Even if the intention is not so clear, the final result is no different with the colonialist by persuasion. A government official assigned there by chance, or a cousin to whom a cousin offers asylum, he may even be a leftist upon arrival and develop irresistibly by the same relentless mechanism into a rude or cunning colonialist. As though it had been enough to cross the sea, as though he had rotted in the heat! The converse applies to native-born colonizers. While the majority cling to their historical opportunity and defend it at all cost, there are some who travel the opposite path, rejecting colonization and, perhaps, leaving the colony. They are for the most part very young people, the most generous ones, the most open ones who, upon leaving adolescence, decide that they do not want to spend their manhood in a colony.

In both cases, the best go away. Either for ethical reasons, not being able to justify profiting from daily injustice, or simply out of pride, because they feel they are of better stuff than the average colonizer, they leave the colony. They set their sights on ambitions and horizons other than those of the colony which, contrary to what is thought, are very limited. In either case, the colony cannot retain the outstanding members of its populations: those who came temporarily and are going back mocking the deception of the colony; those natives who cannot stand rigged games at which it is too easy to become a success without applying one's full capabilities. "The successful colonized are usually superior to Europeans in the same category," admitted a jury foreman to me bitterly. "You can be sure that they deserve it."

The constant removal of the best colonizers explains one of the most frequent characteristics of those who remain in the colony—their mediocrity.

The inconsistency among the prestige, pretentions and responsibilities of a colonialist, combined with the disparity between his true capacity and the results of his work, is too vast. When approaching a colonialist society, one cannot help expecting to find an elite, or at least a selection of the best, most efficient or most reliable technicians. Almost everywhere, those persons occupy, by right or *de facto*, the top posts; they know it and claim esteem and honor because of it. The society of colonizers intends to be a managing society and works hard to give that appearance. The receptions of *délégués* from the mother country are more like those accorded a head of government than those for a *préfet*. The least significant trip involves a series of imperious, backfiring and whistling motorcyclists. Nothing is spared to make an impression on the colonized, the foreigner and, possibly, the colonizer himself.

On examining the situation more closely, one generally finds only men of small stature beyond the pomp or simple pride of the petty colonizer. With practically no knowledge of history, politicians given the task of shaping history, are always taken by surprise or incapable of forecasting events. Specialists responsible for the technical future of a country turn out to be technicians who are behind the time because they are spared from all competition. As far as administrators are concerned, the negligence and indigence of colonial management are well known. It must truthfully be said that better management of a colony hardly forms part of the purposes of colonization.

Since there is no more a colonizer race than there is a colonized race, there certainly must be another explanation for the surprising shortcomings of the rulers of a colony. We have already noted the defection of the best ones; a double defection, of native-born and newcomers. This phenomenon results in a disastrous complement; the mediocre ones remain, and for their whole life. This is because they had not hoped for much. Once settled in, they will be careful not to cede their position unless a better one is proposed to them (which can only happen in a colony). That is why, contrary to what is commonly said, colonial personnel are relatively stable. The promotion of mediocre personnel is not a temporary error but a lasting catastrophe from which the colony never recovers. The birds of passage, even if animated by considerable energy, never succeed in shattering the appearance, or simply the administrative routine, of colonial headquarters.

The gradual selection of the mediocre which necessarily takes place in a colony is further worsened by a restricted recruiting ground. Only the colonizer is called by birth, father to son, uncle to nephew, from cousin to cousin, by an exclusive and racist government to manage the affairs of the city. The governing class, solely of the colonizer group, thus benefits from only negligible inflow of new blood. A kind of etiolation, if one can call it that, is produced by administrative consanguinity.

It is the mediocre citizens who set the general tone of the colony. They are the true partners of the colonized, for it is the mediocre who are most in need of compensation and of colonial life. It is between them and the colonized that the most typical colonial relationships are created. They will hold on so much more tightly to those relationships, to the colonial system, to their status quo, because their entire colonial existence—they have a presentiment of it—depends thereon. They have wagered everything, and for keeps, on the colony.

Even if every colonialist is not mediocre, every colonizer must, in a certain measure, accept the mediocrity of colonial life and the men who thrive on it.

It is also clear that every colonizer must adapt himself to his true situation and the human relationships resulting from it. By having chosen to ratify the colonial system, the colonialist has not really overcome the actual difficulties. The colonial situation thrusts economic, political, and affective facts upon every colonizer against which he may rebel, but which he can never abandon. These facts form the very essence of the colonial system, and soon the colonialist realizes his own ambiguity.

Accepting his role as colonizer, the colonialist accepts the blame implied by that role. This decision in no way brings him permanent peace of mind. On the contrary, the effort he will make to overcome the confusion of his role will give us one of the keys to understanding his ambiguous position. Human relationships in the colony would perhaps have been better if the colonialist had been convinced of his legitimacy. In effect, the problem before the colonizer who accepts is the same as that before the one who refuses. Only their solutions are different; the colonizer who accepts inevitably becomes a colonialist.

Certain features which can be grouped into a coherent whole spring from this assumption of himself and his situation. These related features form *The Usurper's Role* (or, the Nero complex).

As was stated before, accepting the reality of being a colonizer means agreeing to be a nonlegitimate privileged person, that is, a usurper. To be sure, a usurper claims his place and, if need be, will defend it by every means at his disposal. This amounts to saying that at the very time of his triumph, he admits that what triumphs in him is an image which he condemns. His true victory will therefore never be upon him: now he need only record it in the laws and morals. For this he would have to convince the others, if not himself. In other words, to possess victory completely he needs to absolve himself of it and the conditions under which it was attained. This explains his strenuous insistence, strange for a victor, on apparently futile matters. He endeavors to falsify history, he rewrites laws, he would extinguish memories—anything to succeed in transforming his usurpation into legitimacy.

How? How can usurpation try to pass for legitimacy? One attempt can be made by demonstrating the usurper's eminent merits, so eminent that they deserve such compensation. Another is to harp on the usurped's demerits, so deep that they cannot help leading to misfortune. His disquiet and resulting thirst for justification require the usurper to extol himself to the skies and to drive the usurped below the ground at the same time. In effect, these two attempts at legitimacy are actually inseparable.

Moreover, the more the usurped is downtrodden, the more the usurper triumphs and, thereafter, confirms his guilt and establishes his self-condemnation. Thus, the momentum of this mechanism for defense propels itself and worsens as it continues to move. This self-defeating process pushes the usurper to go one step further; to wish the disappearance of the usurped, whose very existence causes him to take the role of usurper, and whose heavier and heavier oppression makes him more and more an oppressor himself. Nero, the typical model of a usurper, is thus brought to persecute Britannicus savagely and to pursue him. But the more he hurts him, the more he coincides with the atrocious role he has chosen for himself. The more he sinks into injustice, the more he hates Britannicus. He seeks to injure the victim who turns Nero into a tyrant. Not content with having taken his throne, Nero tries to ravish his only remaining possession, the love of Junia. It is neither pure jealousy nor perverseness which draws him irresistibly toward the supreme temptation, but rather that inner inevitability or usurpation—moral and physical suppression of the usurped.

In the case of the colonialist, however, the temptation to effect the disappearance of the usurped finds its self-regulation within itself. If he can vaguely desire—perhaps even revealing it—to eliminate the colonized from the roll of the living, it would be impossible for him to do so without eliminating himself. The colonialist's existence is so closely aligned with that of the colonized that he will never be able to overcome the argument which states that misfortune is good for something. With all his power he must disown the colonized while their existence is indispensable to his own. Having chosen to maintain the colonial system, he must contribute more vigor to its defense than would have been needed to dissolve it completely. Having become aware of the unjust relationship which ties him to the colonized, he must continually attempt to absolve himself. He never forgets to make a public show of his own virtues, and will argue with vehemence to appear heroic and great. At the same time his privileges arise just as much from his glory as from degrading the colonized. He will persist in degrading them, using the darkest colors to depict them. If need be, he will act to devalue them, annihilate them. But he can never escape from this circle. The distance which colonization places between him and the colonized must be accounted for and, to justify himself, he increases this distance still further by placing the two figures irretrievably in opposition; his glorious position and the despicable one of the colonized.

This self-justification thus leads to a veritable ideal reconstruction of the two protagonists of the colonial drama. Nothing is easier than to put together the supposed features of those two portraits proposed by the colonialist. For this, a brief stay in a colony, a few conversations, or simply a hasty glance over the press or a so-called colonial novel would suffice.

We shall see that these two images are not without importance. That of the colonized as seen by the colonialist; widely circulated in the colony and often throughout the world (which, thanks to his newspapers and literature, ends up by being echoed to a certain extent in the conduct and, thus, in the true appearance of the colonized). Likewise, the manner in which the colonialist wants to see himself plays a considerable role in the emergence of his final portrait.

For it is not just a case of intellectualizing but the choice of an entire way of life. This man, perhaps a warm friend and affectionate father, who in his native country (by his social condition, his family environment, his natural friendships) could have been a democrat, will surely be transformed into a conservative, reactionary, or even a colonial fascist. He cannot help but approve discrimination and the codification of injustice, he will be delighted at police tortures and, if the necessity arises, will become convinced of the necessity of massacres. Everything will lead him to these beliefs: his new interests, his professional relations, his family ties and bonds of friendship formed in the colony. The mechanism is practically constant. The colonial situation manufactures colonialists, just as it manufactures the colonized.

For it is not without cause that one needs the police and the army to earn one's living or force and injustice to continue to exist. It is not without detriment that one is willing to live permanently with one's guilt. The eulogizing of oneself and one's fellows, the repeated, even earnest, affirmation of the excellence of one's ways and institutions, one's cultural and technical superiority do not erase the fundamental condemnation which every colonialist carries in his heart. If he should try to muffle his own inner voice, everything, every day, would remind him of a contradictory pose: the very sight of the colonized, polite insinuations or sharp accusations by foreigners, confessions by his compatriots in the colony, visits back home where during each trip he finds himself surrounded by a suspicion mixed with envy and condescension. To be sure, he is treated with respect, like all those who hold or share some economic or political power. But there are suggestions that he is a crafty man who knows how to take advantage of a particular situation, whose resources are probably of questionable validity. It is almost as though people are giving him a knowing wink.

Against this accusation, implicit or open, but always there, always in readiness within himself and in others, he defends himself as best he can. Sometimes he stresses the difficulties of his life abroad: the treacherous nature of an insidious climate, the frequency of illnesses, the struggle against unfertile soil, distrust by hostile populations. Other times, furious, aggressive, he reacts clumsily, giving scorn for scorn, accusing his homeland of cowardice and degeneracy. On the other hand, he admits his guilt by proclaiming the riches of living abroad; and after all, why not? He basks in the privileges of his chosen life: easy living, numerous servants, abundant pleasures (impossible in Europe), anachronistic authority —even the low cost of gasoline.

Nothing and no one can give him the high praise he so avidly seeks as compensation: neither the outsider, indifferent at best, but not a dupe or accessory; nor his native land where he is always suspected and often attacked; nor his own daily acts which would ignore the silent revolt of the colonized. In truth, put under accusation by the others, he scarcely believes in his own innocence. Deep within himself, the colonialist pleads guilty.

Under these conditions, it is clear that he does not seriously hope to find within himself the source of that indispensable grandeur, the badge of his rehabilitation. The excesses of his vanity, the too magnificent portrait he paints of himself, betray him more than serve him. He has always been directing attention beyond himself: he seeks this final refuge in his mother country.

His homeland must, indeed, bring together two preliminary conditions. The first is that it relate to a world in which he himself participates if he wants the credits of the mediator to reflect on him. The second is that this world must be totally extraneous to the colonized so that he can never avail himself of it. Miraculously these two conditions are both found in his home country. He will, therefore, call attention to the qualities of his native land—extolling them, exaggerating them—stressing its special traditions, its cultural originality. Thus, at the same time, he establishes his own share in that prosperous world, his natural tie to his homeland. Likewise, he is assured of the impossibility of the colonized sharing in its magnificence.

Furthermore, the colonialist wants to profit every day from this choice, this grace. He presents himself as one of the most perceptive members of the national community, for he is grateful and faithful. He knows, as compared to the citizens back home whose happiness is never threatened, what he owes to his origin. His faithfulness is, however, abstract—his very absence attests to it. It is not soiled by all the trivialities of the daily life of his fellow citizens back home who must gain everything by ingenuity and electoral schemes. His pure fervor for the mother country makes him a true patriot, a fine ambassador, representing its most noble features.

In one sense it is true that he can make people believe it. He loves the most flashy symbols, the most striking demonstrations of the power of his country. He attends all military parades and he desires and obtains frequent and elaborate ones; he contributes his part by dressing up carefully and ostentatiously. He admires the army and its strength, reveres uniforms and covets decorations. Here we overlap what is customarily called power politics, which does not stem only from an economic principle (show your strength if you want to avoid having to use it), but corresponds to a deep necessity of colonial life; to impress the colonized is just as important as to reassure oneself.

Having assigned to his homeland the burden of his own decaying grandeur, he expects it to respond to his hopes. He wants it to merit his confidence, to reflect on him that image of itself which he desires (an ideal which is inaccessible to the colonized and a perfect justification for his own borrowed merits). Often, by dint of hoping, he ends up beginning to believe it. The newly arrived, whose memory is still fresh, speak of their native country with infinitely more accuracy than do veteran colonialists. In their inevitable comparisons between the two countries, the credit and debit columns can still compete. The colonialist appears to have forgotten the living reality of his home country. Over the years he has sculptured, in opposition to the colony, such a monument of his homeland that the colony necessarily appears coarse and vulgar to the novitiate. It is remarkable that even for colonizers born in the colony, that is, reconciled to the sun, the heat and the dry earth, the other scenery looks misty, humid and green. As though their homeland were an essential component of the collective superego of colonizers, its material features become quasi-ethical qualities. It is agreed that mist is intrinsically superior to bright sunshine, as is green to ocher. The mother country thus combines only positive values, good climate, harmonious landscape, social discipline and exquisite liberty, beauty, morality and logic.

It would, nevertheless, be naïve to tell a colonialist that he should go back to that wonderful land, as soon as possible, repairing the error of having left it. Since when does one settle down amidst virtue and beauty? The characteristic of a superego is indeed not to be a part of things, to control from a distance without ever being touched by the prosaic and convulsive behavior of men of flesh and blood. The mother country is so big only because it is beyond the horizon and allows the existence and behavior of the colonialist to be made worthwhile. If he should go home, it would lose its sublime nature, and he would cease to be a superior man. Although he is everything in the colony, the colonialist knows that in his own country he would be nothing; he would go back to being a mediocre man. Indeed, the idea of mother country is relative. Restored to its true self, it would vanish and would at the same time destroy the super-humanity of the colonialist. It is only in a colony, because he possesses a mother country and his fellow inhabitants do not, that a colonialist is feared and admired. Why should he leave the only place in the world where, without being the founder of a city or a great captain, it is still possible to change the names of villages and to bequeath one's name to geography? Without even fearing the simple ridicule or anger of the inhabitants, for their opinion means nothing; where daily one experiences euphorically his power and importance?

It is necessary, then, not only that the home country constitute the remote and never intimately known ideal, but also that this ideal be immutable and sheltered from time; the colonialist requires his homeland to be conservative.

He, of course, is resolutely conservative. It is on just that point that he is most rigid, that he compromises the least. If absolutely necessary, he tolerates criticism of the institutions and ways of the people at home; he is not responsible for the inferior, if he asks for something better. But he is seized with worry and panic each time there is talk of changing the political status. It is only then that the purity of his patriotism is muddled, his indefectible attachment to his motherland shaken. He may go as far as to threaten—Can such things be!—Secession! Which seems contradictory, in conflict with his so well-advertised and, in a certain sense, real patriotism.

But the colonialist's nationalism is truly of a special nature. He directs his attention essentially to that aspect of his native country which tolerates his colonialist existence. A homeland which became democratic, for example, to the point of promoting equality of rights even in the colonies, would also risk abandoning its colonial undertakings. For the colonialist, such a transformation would challenge his way of life and thus become a matter of life or death.

In order that he may subsist as a colonialist, it is necessary that the mother country eternally remain a mother country. To the extent that this depends upon him, it is understandable if he uses all his energy to that end.

Now one can carry this a step further; every colonial nation carries the seeds of fascist temptation in its bosom.

What is fascism, if not a regime of oppression for the benefit of a few? The entire administrative and political machinery of a colony has no other goal. The human relationships have arisen from the severest exploitation, founded on inequality and contempt, guaranteed by police authoritarianism. There is no doubt in the minds of those who have lived through it that colonialism is one variety of fascism. One should not be too surprised by the fact that institutions depending, after all, on a liberal central government can be so different from those in the mother country. This totalitarian aspect which even democratic regimes take on in their colonies is contradictory in appearance only. Being represented among the colonized by colonialists, they can have no other.

It is no more surprising that colonial fascism is not easily limited to the colony. Cancer wants only to spread. The colonialist can only support oppressive and reactionary or, at least, conservative governments. He tends toward that which will maintain the current status of his homeland, or rather that which will more positively assure the framework of oppression. Since it is better for him to forestall than to cure, why should he not be tempted to promote the birth of colonial governments? If one adds that his financial and therefore political means are great, it will be realized that he represents a permanent danger for home government, a pouch of venom forever liable to poison the entire structure of the homeland.

Even if he should never move, the very fact of his living in a colonial system gives rise to uncertainties at home; an alluring example of a political pattern whose difficulties are resolved by the complete servitude of the governed. It is no exaggeration to say that, just as the colonial situation corrupts the European in the colonies, the colonialist is the seed of corruption in the mother country.

The danger and ambiguity of his excessive patriotic ardor are found again, and confirmed, in the more general ambiguity of his relations with his native country. To be sure, he sings its glory and clings to it, even paralyzing it, drowning it if need be. But, at the same time, he harbors deep resentment against the mother country and its citizens.

Up to now we have noted only the privileges of the colonizer with respect to the colonized. Actually, a European in the colonies knows that he is doubly privileged—with respect to the colonized and with respect to the inhabitants of his native land. Colonial advantages also mean that in a comparable position, a government employee earns more, a merchant pays fewer taxes, an industrialist pays less for raw materials and labor, than do their counterparts back home. The comparison does not end there. As well as being tied to the existence of the colonized, colonial privileges are a function of the mother country and its citizens. The colonialist is not unaware that he obliges his home country to maintain an army, and that while the colony is nothing but an advantage for him, it costs the mother country more than it earns for it.

And just as the nature of the relationship between colonizer and colonized is derived from their economic and social relationships, the relationships between the colonizer and the inhabitants of the mother country arise from their comparative situations. The colonizer is not proud of the daily difficulties of his fellow citizen: the taxes which weigh on him alone with his mediocre income. The colonizer returns from his annual trip troubled, displeased with himself and furious with the citizens of his homeland. As always, he had to reply to insinuations or even frank attacks, use the rather unconvincing arguments of the dangers of the African sun and illnesses of the alimentary canal, summon to his rescue the mythology of heroes in a colonial helmet. Nor do they speak the same political language. Each colonialist is naturally further to the right than his counterpart in the homeland. A newly arrived friend was telling me of his naïve astonishment: he did not understand why bowlers, who were Socialists or Radicals back home, were reactionaries or inclined toward fascism in the colony.

Finally, political and economic considerations cause a real antagonism between the colonialist and the resident of his homeland. And in this connection, the colonialist is, after all, correct when he speaks of not feeling at home in his native country. He no longer has the same interests as his compatriots. To a certain extent, he no longer belongs to them.

These exaltation-resentment dialectics uniting the colonialist to his homeland give a peculiar shade to the nature of his love for it. To be sure, he takes pains to present the most glorious image of home, but this maneuver is tainted by everything which he expects of it. Not only that, but if he never slackens his military pomposity, if he multiplies his cajolery, he poorly conceals his anger and vexation. He must unceasingly see to it, intervening if necessary, that his home country continue to maintain the troops which protect him, maintain the political habits which tolerate him, and keep up the appearance which suits him. Colonial budgets will be the price paid by mother countries that are convinced of the debatable grandeur of being mother countries.

Such is the enormity of colonial oppression, however, that this over-evaluation of the mother country is never enough to justify the colonial system. Indeed, the distance between master and servant is never great enough. Almost always, the colonialist also devotes himself to a systematic devaluation of the colonized.

He is fed up with his subject, who tortures his conscience and his life. He tries to dismiss him from his mind, to imagine the colony without the colonized. A witticism which is more serious than it sounds states that "Everything would be perfect . . . if it weren't for the natives." But the colonialist realizes that without the colonized, the colony would no longer have any meaning. This intolerable contradiction fills him with a rage, a loathing, always ready to be loosed on the colonized, the innocent yet

inevitable reason for his drama; and not only if he is
a policeman or government specialist, whose professional habits find unhoped-for possibilities of expansion in the colony. I have been horrified to see peace-
ful public servants and teachers (who are otherwise
courteous and well-spoken) suddenly change into
vociferous monsters for trifling reasons. The most
absurd accusations are directed toward the colonized.
An old physician told me in confidence, with a mixture of surliness and solemnity, that the "colonized
do not know how to breathe"; a professor explained
to me pedantically that "the people here don't know
how to walk; they make tiny little steps which don't
get them ahead." Hence, that impression of stamp-
ing feet which seems characteristic of streets in the
colony. The colonized's devaluation thus extends to
everything that concerns him: to his land, which
is ugly, unbearably hot, amazingly cold, evil smelling;
such discouraging geography that it condemns him to
contempt and poverty, to eternal dependence.

This abasement of the colonized, which is supposed to explain his penury, serves at the same time
as a contrast to the luxury of the colonialist. Those
accusations, those irremediable negative judgments,
are always stated with reference to the mother country, that is (we have already seen by what detour)
with reference to the colonialist himself. Ethical or
sociological, aesthetic or geographic comparisons,
whether explicit and insulting or allusive and dis-

creet, are always in favor of the mother country and the colonialist. This place, the people here, the customs of this country are always inferior—by virtue of an inevitable and pre-established order.

This rejection of the colony and the colonized seriously affects the life and behavior of the colonized. But it also produces a disastrous effect upon the colonialist's conduct. Having thus described the colony, conceding no merits to the colonial community, recognizing neither its traditions, nor its laws, nor its ways, he cannot acknowledge belonging to it himself. He refuses to consider himself a citizen with rights and responsibilities. On the other hand, while he may claim to be indissolubly tied to his native land, he does not live there, does not participate in or react to the collective consciousness of his fellow citizens. The result is that the colonialist is unsure of his true nationality. He navigates between a faraway society which he wants to make his own (but which becomes to a certain degree mythical), and a present society which he rejects and thus keeps in the abstract.

It is not the dryness of the country or the lack of grace of the colonial communities which explain the colonialist's rejection. It is rather because he has not adopted it, or could not adopt it, that the land remains arid and the architecture remains unimaginative in its functionalism. Why does he do nothing about town planning, for example? When he complains about the presence of a bacterially infected lake at the gates of the city, of overflowing sewers or poorly functioning utilities, he seems to forget that he holds power in the government and should assume the blame. Why does he not direct his efforts in a disinterested manner, or is he unable to? Every municipality reflects its inhabitants, guards their immediate and future welfare and their posterity. The colonialist does not plan his future in terms of the colony, for he is there only temporarily and invests only what will bear fruit in his time. The true reason, the principal reason for most deficiencies is that the colonialist never planned to transform the colony into the image of his homeland, nor to remake the colonized in his own image! He cannot allow such an equation—it would destroy the principle of his privileges.

The colonialist always clearly states that this similarity is unthinkable. In fact, achieving this equation is only the vague dream of a humanist from the mother country. But the explanation which the colonialist feels he must give (itself extremely significant) is entirely different. This equality is impossible because of the nature of the colonized. In other words, and this is the characteristic which completes this portrait, the colonialist resorts to racism. It is significant that racism is part of colonialism throughout the world; and it is no coincidence. Racism sums up and symbolizes the fundamental relation which unites colonialist and colonized.

It is, however, not a matter of a doctrinal racism. Besides, that would be difficult; the colonialist likes neither theory nor theorists. He who knows that he is in a bad ideological or ethical position generally boasts of being a man of action, one who draws his lessons from experience. The colonialist has too much difficulty in building his scheme of compensation not to mistrust debates. His racism is as usual to his daily survival as is any other prerequisite for existence. Compared to colonial racism, that of European doctrinaires seems transparent, barren of ideas and, at first sight, almost without passion. A mixture of behaviors and reflexes acquired and practiced since very early childhood, established and measured by education, colonial racism is so spontaneously incorporated in even the most trivial acts and words, that it seems to constitute one of the fundamental patterns of colonialist personality. The frequency of its occurrence, its intensity in colonial relationships, would be astounding if we did not know to what extent it helps the colonialist to live and permits his social introduction. The colonialists are perpetually explaining, justifying and maintaining (by word as well as by deed) the place and fate of their silent partners in the colonial drama. The colonized are thus trapped by the colonial system and the colonialist maintains his prominent role.

Colonial racism is built from three major ideological components: one, the gulf between the culture of the colonialist and the colonized; two, the exploitation of these differences for the benefit of the colonialist; three, the use of these supposed differences as standards of absolute fact.

The first component is the least revealing of the colonialist's mental attitude. To search for differences in features between two peoples is not in itself a racist's characteristic, but it has a definitive function and takes on a particular meaning in a racist context. The colonialist stresses those things which keep him separate, rather than emphasizing that which might contribute to the foundation of a joint community. In those differences, the colonized is always degraded and the colonialist finds justification for rejecting his subjects. But perhaps the most important thing is that once the behavioral feature, or historical or geographical factor which characterizes the colonialist and contrasts him with the colonizer, has been isolated, this gap must be kept from being filled. The colonialist removes the factor from history, time, and therefore possible evolution. What is actually a sociological point becomes labeled as being biological or, preferably, metaphysical. It is attached to the colonized's basic nature. Immediately the

colonial relationship between colonized and colonizer, founded on the essential outlook of the two
protagonists, becomes a definitive category. It is what
it is because they are what they are, and neither one
nor the other will ever change.

Going back to the original purpose of all colonial
policy, there are two illustrations which reveal its
failure to fulfill its promised goals. Contrary to general belief, the colonialist never seriously promoted
the religious conversion of the colonized. The relations between the church (Catholic or Protestant)
and colonialism are more complex than is heard
among thinkers of the left. To be sure, the church
has greatly assisted the colonialist; backing his ventures, helping his conscience, contributing to the acceptance of colonization—even by the colonized. But
this profitable alliance was only an accident for the
church. When colonialism proved to be a deadly,
damaging scheme, the church washed its hands of it
everywhere. Today the church hardly defends the
colonial situations and is actually beginning to attack them. In other words, the church used it as it
used itself, but the latter always held to its own
objective. Conversely, while the colonialist rewarded
the church for its assistance by granting it substantial privileges—land, subsidies and an adequate place
for its role in the colony, he never wished it to succeed in its goal—that is, the conversion of all the
colonized. If he had really favored conversion, he

would have allowed the church to fulfill its dream. Particularly at the beginning of colonization, he enjoyed complete freedom of action, unlimited power to oppress and widespread international support.

But the colonialist could not favor an undertaking which would have contributed to the disappearance of colonial relationships. Conversion of the colonized to the colonizer's religion would have been a step toward assimilation. That is one of the reasons why colonial missions failed.

The second illustration is that there is as little social salvation as there is religious conversion for the colonized. Just as the colonized would not be saved from his condition by religious assimilation, he would not be permitted to rise above his social status to join the colonizer group.

The fact is that all oppression is directed at a human group as a whole and, *a priori,* all individual members of that group are anonymously victimized by it. One often hears that workers—that is all workers, since they are workers—are afflicted by this and that defect and this and that fault. The racist accusation directed at the colonized cannot be anything but collective, and every one of the colonized must be held guilty without exception. It is admitted, however, that there is a possible escape from the oppression of a worker. Theoretically at least, a worker can leave his class and change his status, but within the framework of colonization, nothing can

ever save the colonized. He can never move into the
privileged clan; even if he should earn more money
than they, if he should win all the titles, if he should
enormously increase his power.

We have compared oppression and the colonial
struggle to oppression and the class struggle. The
colonizer-colonized, people-to-people relationship
within nations can, in fact, remind one of the bourgeoisie proletariat relationship within a nation. But
the almost absolutely airtight colonial groupings
must also be mentioned. All the efforts of the colonialist are directed toward maintaining this social
immobility, and racism is the surest weapon for this
aim. In effect, change becomes impossible, and any
revolt would be absurd.

Racism appears then, not as an incidental detail,
but as a consubstantial part of colonialism. It is the
highest expression of the colonial system and one of
the most significant features of the colonialist. Not
only does it establish a fundamental discrimination
between colonizer and colonized, a *sine qua non* of
colonial life, but it also lays the foundation for the
immutability of this life.

The racist tone of each move of both the colonialist and the colonizer is the source of the extraordinary spread of racism in the colonies. And not only
the man on the street: A Rabat psychiatrist dared
tell me, after twenty years' practice, that North

African neuroses were due to the North African spirit.

That spirit or that ethnic grouping or that psychism stems from the institutions of another century, from the absence of technical development, from the necessary political bondage—in short, from the whole drama. It demonstrates clearly that the colonial situation is irremediable and will remain in a state of inertia.

But there is one final act of distortion. The servitude of the colonized seemed scandalous to the colonizer and forced him to explain it away under the pain of ending the scandal and threatening his own existence. Thanks to a double reconstruction of the colonized and himself, he is able both to justify and reassure himself.

Custodian of the values of civilization and history, he accomplishes a mission; he has the immense merit of bringing light to the colonized's ignominious darkness. The fact that this role brings him privileges and respect is only justice; colonization is legitimate in every sense and with all its consequences.

Furthermore, since servitude is part of the nature of the colonized, and domination part of his own, there will be no dénouement. To the delights of rewarded virtue he adds the necessity of natural laws. Colonization is eternal, and he can look to his future without worries of any kind.

After this, everything would be possible and would take on a new meaning. The colonialist could afford to relax, live benevolently and even munificently. The colonized could be only grateful to him for softening what is coming to him. It is here that the astonishing mental attitude called "paternalistic" comes into play. A paternalist is one who wants to stretch racism and inequality farther—once admitted. It is, if you like, a charitable racism—which is not thereby less skillful nor less profitable. For the most generous paternalism revolts as soon as the colonized demands his union rights, for example. If he increases his wages, if his wife looks after the colonized, these are gifts and never duties. If he recognized duties, he would have to admit that the colonized have rights. But it is clear from everything above that he has no duties and the colonized have no rights.

Having founded this new moral order where he is by definition master and innocent, the colonialist would at last have given himself absolution. It is still essential that this order not be questioned by others, and especially not by the colonized.

PART TWO

PORTRAIT OF
THE COLONIZED

Mythical portrait of the colonized

Just as the bourgeoisie proposes an image of the proletariat, the existence of the colonizer requires that an image of the colonized be suggested. These images become excuses without which the presence and conduct of a colonizer, and that of a bourgeois, would seem shocking. But the favored image becomes a myth precisely because it suits them too well.

Let us imagine, for the sake of this portrait and accusation, the often-cited trait of laziness. It seems to receive unanimous approval of colonizers from Liberia to Laos, via the Maghreb. It is easy to see to what extent this description is useful. It occupies an important place in the dialectics exalting the colonizer and humbling the colonized. Furthermore, it is economically fruitful.

Nothing could better justify the colonizer's privileged position than his industry, and nothing could better justify the colonized's destitution than his indolence. The mythical portrait of the colonized therefore includes an unbelievable laziness, and that of the colonizer, a virtuous taste for action. At the same time the colonizer suggests that employing the colonized is not very profitable, thereby authorizing his unreasonable wages.

It may seem that colonization would profit by em-

ploying experienced personnel. Nothing is less true.
A qualified worker existing among the colonizers
earns three or four times more than does the colonized, while he does not produce three or four times
as much, either in quantity or in quality. It is more
advantageous to use three of the colonized than one
European. Every firm needs specialists, of course, but
only a minimum of them, and the colonizer imports
or recruits experts among his own kind. In addition,
there is the matter of the special attention and legal
protection required by a European worker. The colonized, however, is only asked for his muscles; he is
so poorly evaluated that three or four can be taken
on for the price of one European.

From listening to him, on the other hand, one finds
that the colonizer is not so displeased with that laziness, whether supposed or real. He talks of it with
amused affability, he jokes about it, he takes up all
the usual expressions, perfects them, and invents
others. Nothing can describe well enough the extraordinary deficiency of the colonized. He becomes
lyrical about it, in a negative way. The colonized
doesn't let grass grow under his feet, but a tree, and
what a tree! A eucalyptus, an American centenarian
oak! A tree? No, a forest!

But, one will insist, is the colonized truly lazy? To
tell the truth, the question is poorly stated. Besides
having to define a point of reference, a norm, varying from one people to another, can one accuse an

entire people of laziness? It can be suspected of individuals, even many of them in a single group. One can wonder if their output is mediocre, whether malnutrition, low wages, a closed future, a ridiculous conception of a role in society, does not make the colonized uninterested in his work. What is suspect is that the accusation is not directed solely at the farm laborer or slum resident, but also at the professor, engineer or physician who does the same number of hours of work as his colonizer colleagues; indeed, all individuals of the colonized group are accused. Essentially, the independence of the accusation from any sociological or historical conditions makes it suspect.

In fact, the accusation has nothing to do with an objective notation, therefore subject to possible changes, but of an institution. By his accusation the colonizer establishes the colonized as being lazy. He decides that laziness is constitutional in the very nature of the colonized. It becomes obvious that the colonized, whatever he may undertake, whatever zeal he may apply, could never be anything but lazy. This always brings us back to racism, which is the substantive expression, to the accuser's benefit, of a real or imaginary trait of the accused.

It is possible to proceed with the same analysis for each of the features found in the colonized.

Whenever the colonizer states, in his language, that the colonized is a weakling, he suggests thereby that this deficiency requires protection. From this comes the concept of a protectorate. It is in the colonized's own interest that he be excluded from management functions, and that those heavy responsibilities be reserved for the colonizer. Whenever the colonizer adds, in order not to fall prey to anxiety, that the colonized is a wicked, backward person with evil, thievish, somewhat sadistic instincts, he thus justifies his police and his legitimate severity. After all, he must defend himself against the dangerous foolish acts of the irresponsible, and at the same time—what meritorious concern!—protect him against himself! It is the same for the colonized's lack of desires, his ineptitude for comfort, science, progress, his astonishing familiarity with poverty. Why should the colonizer worry about things that hardly trouble the interested party? It would be, he adds with dark and insolent philosophy, doing him a bad turn if he subjected him to the disadvantages of civilization. After all, remember that wisdom is Eastern; let us accept, as he does, the colonized's wretchedness. The same reasoning is also true for the colonized's notorious ingratitude; the colonizer's acts of charity are wasted, the improvements the colonizer has made are not appreciated. It is impossible to save the colonized from this myth—a portrait of wretchedness has been indelibly engraved.

It is significant that this portrait requires nothing else. It is difficult, for instance, to reconcile most of these features and then to proceed to synthesize them objectively. One can hardly see how the colonized can be simultaneously inferior and wicked, lazy and backward.

What is more, the traits ascribed to the colonized are incompatible with one another, though this does not bother his prosecutor. He is depicted as frugal, sober, without many desires and, at the same time, he consumes disgusting quantities of meat, fat, alcohol, anything; as a coward who is afraid of suffering and as a brute who is not checked by any inhibitions of civilization, etc. It is additional proof that it is useless to seek this consistency anywhere except in the colonizer himself. At the basis of the entire construction, one finally finds a common motive; the colonizer's economic and basic needs, which he substitutes for logic, and which shape and explain each of the traits he assigns to the colonized. In the last analysis, these traits are all advantageous to the colonizer, even those which at first sight seem damaging to him.

The point is that the colonized means little to the colonizer. Far from wanting to understand him as he really is, the colonizer is preoccupied with making him undergo this urgent change. The mechanism of this remolding of the colonized is revealing in itself. It consists, in the first place, of a series of negations. The colonized is not this, is not that. He is never considered in a positive light; or if he is, the quality which is conceded is the result of a psychological or ethical failing. Thus it is with Arab hospitality, which is difficult to consider as a negative characteristic. If one pays attention, one discovers that the praise comes from tourists, visiting Europeans, and not colonizers, i.e., Europeans who have settled down in the colony. As soon as he is settled, the European no longer takes advantage of this hospitality, but cuts off intercourse and contributes to the barriers which plague the colonized. He rapidly changes palette to portray the colonized, who becomes jealous, withdrawn, intolerant and fanatical. What happens to the famous hospitality? Since he cannot deny it, the colonizer then brings into play the shadows and describes the disastrous consequences.

This hospitality is a result of the colonized's irresponsibility and extravagance, since he has no notion of foresight or economy. From the wealthy down to the fellah, the festivities are wonderful and bountiful: but what happens afterward? The colonized ruins himself, borrows and finally pays with someone else's money! Does one speak, on the other hand, of the modesty of the colonized's life? Of his not less well known lack of needs? It is no longer a proof of wisdom but of stupidity—as if, then, every recognized or invented trait had to be an indication of negativity.

Thus, one after another, all the qualities which

make a man of the colonized crumble away. The humanity of the colonized, rejected by the colonizer, becomes opaque. It is useless, he asserts, to try to forecast the colonized's actions ("They are unpredictable!" "With them, you never know!"). It seems to him that strange and disturbing impulsiveness controls the colonized. The colonized must indeed be very strange, if he remains so mysterious after years of living with the colonizer.

Another sign of the colonized's depersonalization is what one might call the mark of the plural. The colonized is never characterized in an individual manner; he is entitled only to drown in an anonymous collectivity ("They are this." "They are all the same."). If a colonized servant does not come in one morning, the colonizer will not say that she is ill, or that she is cheating, or that she is tempted not to abide by an oppressive contract. (Seven days a week; colonized domestics rarely enjoy the one day off a week granted to others.) He will say, "You can't count on them." It is not just a grammatical expression. He refuses to consider personal, private occurrences in his maid's life; that life in a specific sense does not interest him, and his maid does not exist as an individual.

Finally, the colonizer denies the colonized the most precious right granted to most men: liberty. Living conditions imposed on the colonized by colonization make no provision for it; indeed, they ignore it. The colonized has no way out of his state of woe—neither a legal outlet (naturalization) nor a religious outlet (conversion). The colonized is not free to choose between being colonized or not being colonized.

What is left of the colonized at the end of this stubborn effort to dehumanize him? He is surely no longer an alter ego of the colonizer. He is hardly a human being. He tends rapidly toward becoming an object. As an end, in the colonizer's supreme ambition, he should exist only as a function of the needs of the colonizer, i.e., be transformed into a pure colonized.

The extraordinary efficiency of this operation is obvious. One does not have a serious obligation toward an animal or an object. It is then easily understood that the colonizer can indulge in such shocking attitudes and opinions. A colonized driving a car is a sight to which the colonizer refuses to become accustomed; he denies him all normality. An accident, even a serious one, overtaking the colonized almost makes him laugh. A machine-gun burst into a crowd of colonized causes him merely to shrug his shoulders. Even a native mother weeping over the death of her son or a native woman weeping for her husband reminds him only vaguely of the grief of a mother or a wife. Those desperate cries, those unfamiliar gestures, would be enough to freeze his compassion even if it were aroused. An author was recently humorously telling us how rebelling natives were driven like game toward huge cages. The fact that someone had conceived and then dared build those cages, and even more, that reporters had been allowed to photograph the fighting, certainly proves that the spectacle had contained nothing human.

Madness for destroying the colonized having originated with the needs of the colonizer, it is not surprising that it conforms so well to them, that it seems to confirm and justify the colonizer's conduct. More surprising, more harmful perhaps, is the echo that it excites in the colonized himself. Constantly confronted with this image of himself, set forth and imposed on all institutions and in every human contact, how could the colonized help reacting to his portrait? It cannot leave him indifferent and remain a veneer which, like an insult, blows with the wind. He ends up recognizing it as one would a detested nickname which has become a familiar description. The accusation disturbs him and worries him even more because he admires and fears his powerful accuser. "Is he not partially right?" he mutters. "Are we not all a little guilty after all? Lazy, because we have so many idlers? Timid, because we let ourselves be oppressed." Willfully created and spread by the colonizer, this mythical and degrading portrait ends up by being accepted and lived with to a certain extent by the colonized. It thus acquires a certain amount of reality and contributes to the true portrait of the colonized.

This process is not unknown. It is a hoax. It is common knowledge that the ideology of a governing class is adopted in large measure by the governed classes. Now, every ideology of combat includes as an integral part of itself a conception of the adversary. By agreeing to this ideology, the dominated classes practically confirm the role assigned to them. This explains, *inter alia,* the relative stability of societies; oppression is tolerated willy-nilly by the oppressed themselves. In colonial relationships, domination is imposed by people upon people but the pattern remains the same. The characterization and role of the colonized occupies a choice place in colonialist ideology; a characterization which is neither true to life, or in itself incoherent, but necessary and inseparable within that ideology. It is one to which the colonized gives his troubled and partial, but undeniable, assent.

There is only a particle of truth in the fashionable notions of "dependency complex," "colonizability," etc. There undoubtedly exists—at some point in its evolution—a certain adherence of the colonized to colonization. However, this adherence is the result of colonization and not its cause. It arises after and not before colonial occupation. In order for the colonizer to be the complete master, it is not enough for him to be so in actual fact, but he must also believe in its legitimacy. In order for that legitimacy to be complete, it is not enough for the colonized to be a slave, he must also accept this role. The bond between colonizer and colonized is thus destructive and creative. It destroys and re-creates the two partners of colonization into colonizer and colonized. One is disfigured into an oppressor, a partial, unpatriotic and treacherous being, worrying only about his privileges and their defense; the other, into an oppressed creature, whose development is broken and who compromises by his defeat.

Just as the colonizer is tempted to accept his part, the colonized is forced to accept being colonized.

Situations
of
the colonized

Since the colonized is presumed a thief, he must in fact be guarded against (being suspect by definition, why should he not be guilty?). Some laundry was stolen (a frequent incident in these sunny lands, where the laundry dries in the open air and mocks those who are naked), and who but the first colonized seen in that vicinity can be guilty? Since it may be he, they go to his home and take him to the police station.

"Some injustice!" retorts the colonizer. "One time out of two, we hit it right. And, in any case, the thief is a colonized; if we don't find him in the first hut, he'll be in the second one."

It would have been too good if that mythical portrait had remained a pure illusion, a look at the colonized which would only have softened the colonizer's bad conscience. However, impelled by the same needs which created it, it cannot fail to be expressed in actual conduct, in active and constructive behavior.

This conduct, which is common to colonizers as a group, thus becomes what can be called a social institution. In other words, it defines and establishes concrete situations which close in on the colonized, weigh on him until they bend his conduct and leave their marks on his face. Generally speaking, these are situations of inadequacy. The ideological aggression which tends to dehumanize and then deceive the colonized finally corresponds to concrete situations which lead to the same result. To be deceived to some extent already, to endorse the myth and then adapt to it, is to be acted upon by it. That myth is furthermore supported by a very solid organization; a government and a judicial system fed and renewed by the colonizer's historic, economic and cultural needs. Even if he were insensitive to calumny and scorn, even if he shrugged his shoulders at insults and jostling, how could the colonized escape the low wages, the agony of his culture, the law which rules him from birth until death?

Just as the colonized cannot escape the colonialist hoax, he could not avoid those situations which create real inadequacy. To a certain extent, the true portrait of the colonized is a function of this relationship. Reversing a previous formula, it can be stated that colonization creates the colonized just as we have seen that it creates the colonizer.

The most serious blow suffered by the colonized is being removed from history and from the community. Colonization usurps any free role in either war or peace, every decision contributing to his destiny and that of the world, and all cultural and social responsibility.

It is true that discouraged citizens of free countries tell themselves that they have no voice in the nation's affairs, that their actions are useless, that their voice is not heard, and that the elections are fixed. Such people claim that the press and radio are in the hands of a few, that they cannot prevent war, or demand peace, or even obtain from their elected representatives that for which they were sent to parliament. However, they at least immediately recognize that they possess the right to do so; the potential if not the effective power; that they are deceived or weary, but not enslaved. They try to believe they are free men, momentarily vanquished by hoaxes or stunned by demagogy. Driven beyond the boiling point, they are seized by sudden anger, break their paper chains and upset the politicians' little calculations. These people proudly remember those periodic and just storms! Thinking it over, they may feel guilty for not revolting more often; after all, they are responsible for their own freedom and if, because of fatigue or weakness or skepticism, they do not use it, they deserve their punishment.

The colonized, on the other hand, feels neither responsible nor guilty nor skeptical, for he is out of the game. He is in no way a subject of history any more. Of course, he carries its burden, often more cruelly than others, but always as an object. He has forgotten how to participate actively in history and no longer even asks to do so. No matter how briefly colonization may have lasted, all memory of freedom seems distant; he forgets what it costs or else he no longer dares to pay the price for it. How else can one explain how a garrison of a few men can hold out in a mountain post? How a handful of often arrogant colonizers can live in the midst of a multitude of colonized? The colonizers themselves are amazed, and it follows that they accuse the colonized of cowardice. Actually, the accusation is too easy; they know very well that if they were in danger, their lonely position would quickly be changed. All the resources of science—telephone, telegraph, and airplane—would be placed at their disposal and, within a few minutes, terrible weapons of defense and destruction. For each colonizer killed, hundreds or thousands of the colonized have been or would be exterminated. That experience has occurred often enough—perhaps incited—for the colonized to be convinced of the inevitable and heinous punishment. Everything has been brought into play to destroy his courage to die and face the sight of blood.

It is even more clear that if it is really a matter of inadequacy involved, born of a situation and of the will of the colonizer, it is only that and not some congenital inability to assume a role in history. The severity of the laws attest to the difficulty of conditioning the colonized to feel inadequate. While it is pardonable for the colonizer to have his little arsenals, the discovery of even a rusty weapon among the colonized is cause for immediate punishment. The Arab *fantasia* has become nothing more than the act of a trained animal which is asked to roar, as he used to, to frighten the guests. But the animal roars extremely well; and nostalgia for arms is always present, and is part of all ceremonies in Africa, from north to south. The lack of implements of war appears proportional to the size of the colonialist forces; the most isolated tribes are still the first to pick up their weapons. That is not a proof of savagery, but only evidence that the conditioning is not sufficiently maintained.

That is also why the experience of the last war was so decisive. It did not only, as has been stated, imprudently teach the colonized the technique of guerilla warfare, but also it reminded them of the possibility of aggressive and free action. The European governments which, after that war, prohibited the showing of certain movies of resistance in colonial theaters were not wrong from their point of view. In objection to this, it was stated that American Westerns, gangster pictures and war propaganda strips had already shown how to use a revolver or tommy-gun. That argument was not enough. The significance of resistance films is entirely different. They show that poorly armed or even unarmed oppressed people did dare attack their oppressors.

When the first disturbances broke out in the colonies, those who did not understand their meaning were consoled by the fact that there were so few active fighters. The colonized, it is true, hesitates before taking his destiny in his hands. But the meaning of the event was so much greater than its arithmetical weight! The rebels were laughed at because of their insistence on wearing khaki uniforms. Obviously, they hoped to be considered soldiers and treated in accordance with the rules of war. There is profound meaning to this emphatic desire, as it was by this tactic that they laid claim to and wore the dress of history; and, unfortunately, history today wears a military uniform.

As mentioned before, the same goes for community affairs. "They are not capable of governing themselves," says the colonizer. "That is why," he explains, "I don't let them and will never let them, enter the government."

The fact is that the colonized does not govern. Being kept away from power, he ends up by losing both interest and feeling for control. How could he be interested in something from which he is so resolutely excluded? Among the colonized few men are suitable for government. How could such a long absence from autonomous government give rise to skill? Can the colonizer succeed in barring the colonized from future participation in government by cheating him from this role in the present?

Since the colonized's organizations have nationalistic claims, it is often concluded that the colonized are chauvinistic. Nothing is less true. What is involved, on the contrary, is an ambition and a form of

mob psychology which appeals to passionate motives. Except among the militants of this national
renaissance, the usual signs of chauvinism—aggressive love for the flag, use of patriotic songs, fervent
feeling of belonging to the same national organization—are rare among the colonized. It is repeated
that the colonization precipitated the awakening of
national consciousness of the colonized. One could
state equally well that it moderated the tempo of this
awareness by keeping the colonized apart from the
true conditions of contemporary citizenship. It is not
a coincidence that colonized peoples are the last to
awaken to national consciousness.

The colonized enjoys none of the attributes of
citizenship; neither his own, which is dependent, con-
tested and smothered, nor that of the colonizer. He
can hardly adhere to one or claim the other. Not
having his just place in the community, not enjoying
the rights of a modern citizen, not being subject to
his normal duties, not voting, not bearing the burden
of community affairs, he cannot feel like a true citizen. As a result of colonization, the colonized almost
never experiences nationality and citizenship, except
privately. Nationally and civically he is only what
the colonizer is not.

This social and historical mutilation gives rise to
the most serious consequences. It contributes to
bringing out the deficiencies in the other aspects of
the colonized's life and, by a countereffect which is

frequent in human processes, it is itself fed by the colonized's other infirmities.

Not considering himself a citizen, the colonized likewise loses all hope of seeing his son achieve citizenship. Before long, renouncing citizenship himself, he no longer includes it in his plans, eliminates it from his paternal ambitions, and allows no place for it in his teachings. Nothing therefore suggests to the young colonized the self-assurance or pride of his citizenship. He will expect nothing more from it and will not be prepared to assume its responsibilities. (Obviously, there is likewise nothing in his school education, in which references to the community and nation are always in terms of the colonizing nation.) This educational void, a result of social inadequacy, thus perpetuates that same inadequacy, damaging one of the essential dimensions of the colonized individual.

Later, as an adolescent, it is with difficulty that he conceives vaguely, if at all, of the only way out of a disastrous family situation . . . revolt. The ring is tightly sealed. Revolt against his father and family is a wholesome act and an indispensable one for self-achievement. It permits him to start his adult life—a new unhappy and happy battle—among other men. The conflict of generations can and must be resolved by social conflict; conversely, it is thus a factor in movement and progress. The young generations find the solution to their problems in collective move-

ments. By choosing a movement, they accelerate it. It
is necessary, of course, that that movement be possible. Now, into what kind of life and social dynamic
do we emerge? The colony's life is frozen; its structure is both corseted and hardened. No new role is
open to the young man, no invention is possible.
The colonizer admits this with a now classical
euphemism: He respects, he proclaims, the ways and
customs of the colonized. And, to be sure, he cannot
help respecting them, be it by force. Since any change
would have to be made against colonization, the
colonizer is led to favor the least progressive features.
He is not solely responsible for this mummification
of the colonized society; he demonstrates relatively
good faith when he maintains that it is independent
by its own will. It derives largely, however, from the
colonial situation. Not being master of its destiny,
not being its own legislator, not controlling its organization, colonized society can no longer adapt its
institutions to its grievous needs. But it is those needs
which practically shape the organizational face of
every normal society. It is under their constant pressure that the political and administrative face of
France has been gradually changing over the centuries. However, if the discord becomes too sharp,
and harmony becomes impossible to attain under
existing legal forms, the result is either to revolt or
to be calcified.

Colonized society is a diseased society in which internal dynamics no longer succeed in creating new structures. Its century-hardened face has become nothing more than a mask under which it slowly smothers and dies. Such a society cannot dissolve the conflicts of generations, for it is unable to be transformed. The revolt of the adolescent colonized, far from resolving into mobility and social progress, can only sink into the morass of colonized society—unless there is a total revolution. But we shall return to that later.

Sooner or later then, the potential rebel falls back on the traditional values. This explains the astonishing survival of the colonized's family. The colonial superstructure has real value as a refuge. It saves the colonized from the despair of total defeat and, in return, it finds confirmation in a constant inflow of new blood. The young man will marry, will become a devoted father, reliable brother, responsible uncle and, until he takes his father's place, a respectful son. Everything has gone back into the order of things. Revolt and conflict have ended in a victory for the parents and tradition.

But it is a pyrrhic victory. Colonized society has not taken even half a step forward; for the young man, it is an internal catastrophe. He will remain glued to that family which offers him warmth and tenderness but which simultaneously absorbs, clutches and emasculates him. Doesn't the community require the full duties of citizenship? Wouldn't it refuse them to him if he should still try to claim them? Doesn't it grant him few rights and prohibit him from participating in all national life? Actually, he no longer desperately needs them. His correct place, always reserved in the soft warmth of clan reunions, satisfies him. He would be afraid to leave it. With good grace now, he submits, as do the others, to his father's authority and prepares to replace him. The model is a weak one. His universe is that of the vanquished. But what other way out is there? By a curious paradox, his father is simultaneously weak and possessive. The young man is ready to assume his role of the colonized adult—that is, to accept being an oppressed creature.

The same goes for the indisputable hold of a deep-rooted and formal religion. Complacently, missionaries depict this formality as an essential feature of non-Christian religions. Thus they suggest that the only way to escape from one would be to pass over to the next closest one. Actually, all religions have moments of coercive formality and moments of indulgent flexibility. It remains to be explained why a given group, at a given period in its history, goes through a certain stage. Why such hollow rigidity in the religions of the colonized?

It would be useless to construct a religious psychology which is peculiar to the colonized or to invoke that all-explaining nature which is attributed to them. While they give a certain amount of attention to religion, one seldom notices excessive religious zeal among the colonized. It seems to me that the explanation is parallel to that of family control. It is not an original psychology which explains the importance of the family, nor is it the intensity of family life which explains the state of social structures. It is rather the impossibility of enjoying a complete social life which maintains vigor in the family and pulls the individual back to that more restricted cell, which saves and smothers him. At the same time, the entire condition of the colonized institutions takes into account the excessive weight of religion.

With its institutional network, its collective and periodic holidays, religion constitutes another refuge value, both for the individual and for the group. For the individual, it is one of the rare paths of retreat; for the group, it is one of the rare manifestations which can protect its original existence. Since colonized society does not possess national structures and cannot conceive of a historical future for itself, it must be content with the passive sluggishness of its present. It must withdraw even that present from the conquering invasion of colonization which gives it prestige with the young generations. Formalism, of which religious formality is only one aspect, is the cyst into which colonial society shuts itself and hardens, degrading its own life in order to save it. It is a spontaneous action of self-defense, a means of safeguarding the collective consciousness without which a people quickly cease to exist. Under the conditions of colonial dependence, religious emancipation, like the breakup of the family, would have involved a serious risk of dying by itself.

The calcified colonized society is therefore the consequence of two processes having opposite symptoms: encystment originating internally and a corset imposed from outside. Both phenomena have one common factor, contact with colonization. They converge in the social and historical catalepsy of the colonized.

As long as he tolerates colonization, the only possible alternatives for the colonized are assimilation or petrifaction. Assimilation being refused him, as we shall see, nothing is left for him but to live isolated from his age. He is driven back by colonization and, to a certain extent, lives with that situation. Planning and building his future are forbidden. He must therefore limit himself to the present, and even that present is cut off and abstract.

We should add that he draws less and less from his past. The colonizer never even recognized that he had one; everyone knows that the commoner whose origins are unknown has no history. Let us ask the colonized himself: who are his folk heroes? his great popular leaders? his sages? At most, he may be able to give us a few names, in complete disorder, and fewer and fewer as one goes down the generations. The colonized seems condemned to lose his memory.

Memory is not purely a mental phenomenon. Just as the memory of an individual is the fruit of his history and physiology, that of a people rests upon its institutions. Now the colonized's institutions are dead or petrified. He scarcely believes in those which continue to show some signs of life and daily confirms their ineffectiveness. He often becomes ashamed of these institutions, as of a ridiculous and overaged monument.

All effectiveness and social dynamics, on the other hand, seem monopolized by the colonizer's institutions. If the colonized needs help, it is to them that he applies. If he does something wrong, it is by them that he is punished. When a man of authority happens to wear a tarboosh, he has an evasive glance and abrupt manners, as though he wanted to forestall any challenge, as though he were under the colonizer's constant surveillance. Suppose the community has a festival. It is the colonizer's holiday, a religious one perhaps, and is celebrated brilliantly—Christmas and Joan of Arc, Carnival and Bastille Day. It is the colonizer's armies which parade, the very ones which crushed the colonized and keep him in his place.

Naturally, by virtue of his formalism, the colonized observes all his religious holidays. These holidays are located at the beginning of history, rather than in history. From the time they were instituted, nothing else has happened in the life of that people. That is, nothing peculiar to their own existence which deserves to be retained by the collective consciousness and celebrated. Nothing except a great void.

Finally, the few material traces of that past are slowly erased, and the future remnants will no longer carry the stamp of the colonized group. The few statues which decorate the city represent (with incredible scorn for the colonized who pass by them every day) the great deeds of colonization. The buildings are patterned after the colonizer's own favorite designs; the same is true of the street names, which recall the faraway provinces from which he came. Occasionally, the colonizer starts a neo-Eastern style, just as the colonized imitates European style. But it is only exoticism (like old guns and antique chests) and not a renaissance; the colonized himself only avoids his own past.

By what else is the heritage of a people handed down? By the education which it gives to its children, and by language, that wonderful reservoir constantly enriched with new experiences. Traditions and acquirements, habits and conquests, deeds and acts of previous generations are thus bequeathed and recorded in history.

However, the very great majority of colonized children are in the streets. And he who has the wonderful good luck to be accepted in a school will not be saved nationally. The memory which is assigned him is certainly not that of his people. The history which is taught him is not his own. He knows who Colbert or Cromwell was, but he learns nothing about Khaznadar; he knows about Joan of Arc, but not about El Kahena. Everything seems to have taken place out of his country. He and his land are nonentities or exist only with reference to the Gauls, the Franks or the Marne. In other words, with reference to what he is not: to Christianity, although he is not a Christian; to the West which ends under his nose, at a line which is even more insurmountable than it is imaginary. The books talk to him of a world which in no way reminds him of his own; the little boy is called Toto and the little girl, Marie; and on winter evenings Marie and Toto walk home along snow-covered paths, stopping in front of a chestnut vendor. His teachers do not follow the same pattern as his father; they are not his wonderful and redeeming successors like every other teacher in the world. They are something else. There is no communication either from child to teacher or (admittedly all too often) from teacher to child, and the child notices this perfectly well. One of my former schoolmates told me that literature, art and philosophy had remained foreign to him, as though pertaining to a theoretical world divorced from reality. It was only after a long visit to Paris that he could really begin to absorb them.

If communication finally takes place, it is not without its dangers. The teacher and school represent a world which is too different from his family environment. In both cases, far from preparing the adolescent to find himself completely, school creates a permanent duality in him.

The colonized is saved from illiteracy only to fall into linguistic dualism. This happens only if he is lucky, since most of the colonized will never have the good fortune to suffer the tortures of colonial bilingualism. They will never have anything but their native tongue; that is, a tongue which is neither written nor read, permitting only uncertain and poor oral development.

Granted, small groups of academicians persist in developing the language of their people, perpetuating it through scholarly pursuits into the splendors of the past. But its subtle forms bear no relationship to everyday life and have become obscure to the man on the street. The colonized considers those venerable scholars relics and thinks of them as sleepwalkers who are living in an old dream.

If only the mother tongue was allowed some influence on current social life, or was used across the counters of government offices, or directed the postal service; but this is not the case. The entire bureaucracy, the entire court system, all industry hears and uses the colonizer's language. Likewise, highway markings, railroad station signs, street signs and receipts make the colonized feel like a foreigner in his own country.

In the colonial context, bilingualism is necessary. It is a condition for all culture, all communication and all progress. But while the colonial bilinguist is saved from being walled in, he suffers a cultural catastrophe which is never completely overcome.

The difference between native language and cultural language is not peculiar to the colonized, but colonial bilingualism cannot be compared to just any linguistic dualism. Possession of two languages is not merely a matter of having two tools, but actually means participation in two psychical and cultural realms. Here, the two worlds symbolized and conveyed by the two tongues are in conflict; they are those of the colonizer and the colonized.

Furthermore, the colonized's mother tongue, that which is sustained by his feelings, emotions and dreams, that in which his tenderness and wonder are expressed, thus that which holds the greatest emotional impact, is precisely the one which is the least valued. It has no stature in the country or in the concert of peoples. If he wants to obtain a job, make a place for himself, exist in the community and the world, he must first bow to the language of his masters. In the linguistic conflict within the colonized, his mother tongue is that which is crushed. He himself sets about discarding this infirm language, hiding it from the sight of strangers. In short, colonial bilingualism is neither a purely bilingual situation in which an indigenous tongue coexists with a purist's language (both belonging to the same world of feeling), nor a simple polyglot richness benefiting from an extra but relatively neuter alphabet; it is a linguistic drama.

Some express wonder at the fact that the colonized does not have a living literature in his own language. Why should he turn to literature, considering that he disdains it? Similarly, he turns away from his music, the plastic arts and, in effect, his entire traditional culture. His linguistic ambiguity is the symbol and one of the major causes of his cultural ambiguity. The position of a colonized writer is a perfect illustration of this. The material conditions of the existence of the colonized would suffice to explain the rarity of writers. The excessive poverty of the majority drastically reduces the probability of finding a budding and developing writer. However, history shows us that only one privileged class is enough to provide an entire people with artists. The fact is that the role of a colonized writer is too difficult to sustain. He incarnates a magnified vision of all the ambiguities and impossibilities of the colonized.

Suppose that he has learned to manage his language to the point of re-creating it in written works; for whom shall he write, for what public? If he persists in writing in his language, he forces himself to speak before an audience of deaf men. Most of the people are uncultured and do not read any language, while the bourgeoisie and scholars listen only to that of the colonizer. Only one natural solution is left; to write in the colonizer's language. In this case, of course, he is only changing dilemmas.

He must, in either case, overcome his handicap. Although a colonial bilinguist has the advantage of knowing two tongues, he wastes much of his imagination and energy in attempting to achieve a proficiency that will never be fully realized. This is another explanation of the slow birth of colonial literature. After this there re-emerges the ambiguity of the colonized writer in a new but even more serious form.

It is a curious fate to write for a people other than one's own, and it is even stranger to write to the conquerors of one's people. Wonder was expressed at the acrimony of the first colonized writers. Do they forget that they are addressing the same public whose tongue they have borrowed? However, the writer is neither unconscious, nor ungrateful, nor insolent. As soon as they dare speak, what will they tell just those people, other than of their malaise and revolt? Could words of peace or thoughts of gratitude be expected from those who have been suffering from a loan that compounds so much interest? For a loan which, besides, will never be anything but a loan. We are here, it is true, putting aside fact for conjecture. But it is so easy to read, so obvious. The emergence of a literature of a colonized people, the development of consciousness by North African writers for example, is not an isolated occurrence. It is part of the development of the self-consciousness of an entire human group. The fruit is not an accident or miracle of a plant but a sign of its maturity. At most, the surging of the colonized artist is slightly ahead of the development of collective consciousness in which he participates and which he hastens by participating in it. And the most urgent claim of a group about to revive is certainly the liberation and restoration of its language.

Indeed, if I express wonder, it is that anyone wonders. Only that language would allow the colonized to resume contact with his interrupted flow of time and to find again his lost continuity and that of his history. Is the French language only a precise and efficient instrument? Or is it that miraculous chest in which are heaped up discoveries and victories, writers and moralists, philosophers and scholars, heroes and adventurers, in which the treasures of the intellect and of the French soul are transformed into one single legend?

The colonized writer, having succeeded after much effort in being able to use European languages—those of the colonizers, let us not forget—can use them only to clamor for his own. That is not a question of incoherence or blind resentment, but a necessity. Were he not to do it, his entire people would eventually step in. It is an objective dynamism which he feeds, to be sure, but which nourishes him and would continue without him. By so doing, he contributes toward the liquidation of his drama as a man, and he confirms and accentuates his drama as a writer. In order to reconcile his destiny with himself, he could attempt to write in his mother tongue. But such apprenticeship is not repeated during manhood. The colonized writer is condemned to live his renunciations to the bitter end. The problem can be concluded in only two ways: by the natural death of colonized literature; the following generations, born in liberty, will write spontaneously in their newly found language. Without waiting that long, a second possibility can tempt the writer; to decide to join the literature of the mother country. Let us leave aside the ethical problems raised by such an attitude. It is the suicide of colonized literature; in either prospect (the only difference being in the date) colonized literature in European languages appears condemned to die young.

Everything takes place as though contemporary colonization were a historical mistake. By its inherent inevitability and by egotism, it apparently has failed completely and has polluted everything which it has touched. It has decayed the colonizer and destroyed the colonized.

In order to triumph, colonization wanted to serve only its own interests. But, by pushing aside the colonized man, through whom alone it could have exalted the colony, it condemned itself to remain foreign to it and thus of necessity transitory.

It is nevertheless accountable only to itself for its suicide. More unpardonable is its historic crime toward the colonized, dropping him off by the side of the road—outside of our time.

The question of whether the colonized, if let alone, would have advanced at the same pace as other peoples has no great significance. To be perfectly truthful, we have no way of knowing. It is possible that he might not. The colonial factor is certainly not the only one which explains the backwardness of a people. All countries have not followed the same tempo as that of America or England; each had its own special causes of delay and its own restraints. However, each one traveled according to its own pace and along its own path. Furthermore, can one justify the historical misfortune of a people by the difficulties of another? The colonized peoples are not the only victims of history, but the historical misfortune peculiar to the colonized was colonization.

To this same spurious problem, the question which disturbs many people returns. Didn't the colonized nonetheless profit by colonization? Did the colonizer not open roads, build hospitals and schools? This reservation amounts to saying that colonization was positive after all; for without it, there would have been neither roads, nor hospitals, nor schools. How

do we know? Why must we suppose that the colonized would have remained frozen in the state in
which the colonizer found him? We could just as
well put forward the opposite view. If colonization
had not taken place, there would have been more
schools and more hospitals. If Tunisian history were
better known, it would be realized that the country
was then in full pregnancy. After having shut the
colonized out of history and having forbidden him
all development, the colonizer asserts his fundamental and complete immobility.

Besides, that objection disturbs only those who are
inclined to be disturbed. After decades of colonization, the multitude of children in the streets is greatly
in excess of those in the classrooms; the number of
hospital beds is pitiful compared to the number of
sick; the purpose of the highway system is without
regard to the needs of the colonized—but absolutely
in line with those of the colonizer. For so little gain,
colonization was truly not indispensable. Is it daring
to suppose that the Tunisia of 1952 would have been,
in any event, very different from that of 1881? After
all, domination is not the only possible method of
influence and exchange among people. Other small
countries have transformed themselves greatly without being colonized. Thus a number of countries of
Central Europe. . . .

But our listener has been smiling skeptically.
"Yes, but it isn't the same thing."

"Why not? You mean, don't you, that those countries are populated by Europeans?"

"Well—yes!"

"There you are, sir! You are just simply a racist."

Of course, this brings us back to the fundamental
bias. Europeans conquered the world because their
nature was predisposed to it, while non-Europeans
were colonized because their nature condemned them
to it.

But let's be serious and drop right here both racism
and this urge to rewrite history. Let us even put aside
the problem of initial responsibility for colonization.
Was it the result of capitalistic expansion or an acci-
dental venture by voracious businessmen? In the final
analysis, all that is not important. What does count
is the present reality of colonization and the colonized. We have no idea what the colonized would
have been without colonization, but we certainly see
what has happened as a result of it. To subdue and
exploit, the colonizer pushed the colonized out of the
historical and social, cultural and technical current.
What is real and verifiable is that the colonized's
culture, society and technology are seriously dam-
aged. He has not acquired new ability and a new
culture. One patent result of colonization is that
there are no more colonized artists and not yet any
colonized technicians. It is true that there also exists
a technical inadequacy among the colonized. "Arab
work," says the colonizer disdainfully. But far from

finding an excuse for his conduct and a point of comparison in his favor, he should see in it his own guilt. It is true that the colonized do not know how to work. But where were they taught, who taught them modern techniques? Where are the professional schools and centers of apprenticeship?

I sometimes hear it said, "You put too much emphasis on industrial methods. What about handicrafts? Look at that table made with white wood: why is it made of wood taken from crates? Poorly finished, too, badly planed, neither painted nor polished." Yes, of course, that description is correct. The only decent feature in those tea tables is their shape—a centuries-old gift of tradition to the handicraftsman. As for the rest, it is the demand that inspires creation. For whom are those tables made? The buyer cannot afford to pay for those extra strokes with a plane, nor for varnish, nor for paint. So they remain disjointed boards from crates, with the nail holes still open.

What is clear is that colonization weakens the colonized and that all those weaknesses contribute to one another. Nonindustrialization and the absence of technical development in the country lead to a slow economic collapse of the colonized. This collapse threatens the standard of living of the colonized, keeping the technician from existing and the artisan from perfecting himself and his creations. The final causes of the collapse are rejection of the

colonizer who enriches himself further by selling raw
materials rather than competing with industry in the
home country. In addition to this, the system works
within a vicious circle and acquires a calamitous
autonomy. Had more apprenticeship centers and
even universities been open, they would not have
saved the colonized; who, upon leaving them, would
not have found a way to apply their training. In a
country within which everything is lacking, the few
colonized engineers who were able to obtain degrees
are used as bureaucrats or instructors. Colonized society does not have a direct need for technicians and
does not create one. But woe to him who is not indispensable! The colonized laborer is interchangeable,
so why pay him what he is really worth? Besides, as
our times and our history become more and more tech-
nical-minded; the colonized's technical backwardness
increases and seems to justify the scorn which it gen-
erates. This backwardness concretely shows the distance separating him from the colonizer. It is not untrue that the technical distance is partly responsible
for the lack of understanding between the two partners. The general standard of living of the colonized
is often so low that contact is almost impossible. One
gets out of it by speaking of the colony's medieval-
ism. One can go on like that for a long time. Enjoyment of technical advances creates technological traditions. An ordinary Frenchman or ordinary Italian
has the opportunity of tinkering with a motor or a

radio, and is surrounded by products of technology. Many colonized don't even come near the least-complicated machines until they leave their fathers' homes. How can they have a taste for mechanized civilization and a feeling for machinery?

Everything in the colonized is deficient, and everything contributes to this deficiency—even his body, which is poorly fed, puny and sick. Many lengthy discussions would be saved if, in the beginning, it was agreed that there is this wretchedness—collective, permanent, immense. Simple and plain biological wretchedness, chronic hunger of an entire people, malnutrition and illness. Of course, from a distance, that remains a bit abstract, and an extraordinary imagination would be required. I remember that day when the "Tunisienne Automobile" taking us south stopped in the midst of a crowd whose mouths were smiling, but whose eyes, almost all eyes, were watery; I looked uneasily for a nondiseased glance on which to rest my own. Tuberculosis and syphilis, and those skeletonlike and naked bodies passing between the chairs of the cafés like living dead, sticky as flies, the flies of our remorse. . . .

"Oh, no!" cries our questioner. "That poverty was there before! We found it there when we arrived!"

Granted. (Indeed, what is more, the slumdweller is often a dispossessed fellah.) But how could a social system which perpetuates such distress—even supposing that it does not create it—endure for long? How can one dare compare the advantages and disadvantages of colonization? What advantages, even if a thousand times more important, could make such internal and external catastrophes acceptable?

The two answers
of
the colonized

The body and face of the colonized are not a pretty sight. It is not without damage that one carries the weight of such historical misfortune. If the colonizer's face is the odious one of an oppressor, that of his victim certainly does not express calm and harmony. The colonized does not exist in accordance with the colonial myth, but he is nevertheless recognizable. Being a creature of oppression, he is bound to be a creature of want.

How can one believe that he can ever be resigned to the colonial relationship; that face of suffering and disdain allotted to him? In all of the colonized there is a fundamental need for change. For the colonizers to be unconscious of this need means that either their lack of understanding of the colonial system is immense or that their blind selfishness is more than readily believable. To assert, for instance, that the colonized's claims are the acts of a few intellectuals or ambitious individuals, of deception or self-interest, is a perfect example of projection: an explanation of others in terms of one's own interests. The colonized's refusal resembles a surface phenomenon, but it actually derives from the very nature of the colonial situation.

The middle-class colonized suffers most from bilingualism. The intellectual lives more in cultural anguish, and the illiterate person is simply walled into his language and rechews scraps of oral culture. Those who understand their fate become impatient and no longer tolerate colonization. They only express the common misfortune. If not, why would they be so quickly heard, so well understood and obeyed?

If one chooses to understand the colonial system, he must admit that it is unstable and its equilibrium constantly threatened. One can be reconciled to every situation, and the colonized can wait a long time to live. But, regardless of how soon or how violently the colonized rejects his situation, he will one day begin to overthrow his unlivable existence with the whole force of his oppressed personality.

The two historically possible solutions are then tried in succession or simultaneously. He attempts either to become different or to reconquer all the dimensions which colonization tore away from him.

The first attempt of the colonized is to change his condition by changing his skin. There is a tempting model very close at hand—the colonizer. The latter suffers from none of his deficiencies, has all rights, enjoys every possession and benefits from every prestige. He is, moreover, the other part of the comparison, the one that crushes the colonized and keeps him in servitude. The first ambition of the colonized is to become equal to that splendid model and to resemble him to the point of disappearing in him.

By this step, which actually presupposes admiration for the colonizer, one can infer approval of colonization. But by obvious logic, at the very moment when the colonized best adjusts himself to his fate, he rejects himself with most tenacity. That is to say that he rejects, in another way, the colonial situation. Rejection of self and love of another are common to all candidates for assimilation. Moreover, the two components of this attempt at liberation are closely tied. Love of the colonizer is subtended by a complex of feelings ranging from shame to self-hate.

The extremism in that submission to the model is already revealing. A blonde woman, be she dull or anything else, appears superior to any brunette. A product manufactured by the colonizer is accepted with confidence. His habits, clothing, food, architecture are closely copied, even if inappropriate. A mixed marriage is the extreme expression of this audacious leap.

This fit of passion for the colonizer's values would not be so suspect, however, if it did not involve such a negative side. The colonized does not seek merely to enrich himself with the colonizer's virtues. In the name of what he hopes to become, he sets his mind on impoverishing himself, tearing himself away from his true self. The crushing of the colonized is included among the colonizer's values. As soon as the colonized adopts those values, he similarly adopts his own condemnation. In order to free himself, at least so he believes, he agrees to destroy himself. This phenomenon is comparable to Negrophobia in a Negro, or anti-Semitism in a Jew. Negro women try desperately to uncurl their hair, which keeps curling back, and torture their skin to make it a little whiter. Many Jews would, if they could, tear out their souls—that soul which, they are told, is irremediably bad. People have told the colonized that his music is like mewing of cats, and his painting like sugar syrup. He repeats that his music is vulgar and his painting disgusting. If that music nevertheless moves him, excites him more than the tame Western exercises, which he finds cold and complicated, if that unison of singing and slightly intoxicating colors gladdens his eye, it is against his will. He becomes indignant with himself, conceals it from strangers' eyes or makes strong statements of repugnance that are comical. The women of the bourgeoisie prefer a mediocre jewel from Europe to the purest jewel of their tradition. Only the tourists express wonder before the products of centuries-old craftsmanship. The point is that whether Negro, Jew or colonized, one must resemble the white man, the non-Jew, the colonizer. Just as many people avoid showing off their poor relations, the colonized in the throes of assimilation hides his past, his traditions, in fact all his origins which have become ignominious.

Those internal convulsions and contortions could

have attained their goal. At the end of a long, painful process, one certainly full of conflict, the colonized would perhaps have dissolved into the midst of the colonizers. There is no problem which the erosion of history cannot resolve. It is a question of time and generations. There is, however, one condition— that it not contain contradictory ideas. Well, within the colonial framework, assimilation has turned out to be impossible.

The candidate for assimilation almost always comes to tire of the exorbitant price which he must pay and which he never finishes owing. He discovers with alarm the full meaning of his attempt. It is a dramatic moment when he realizes that he has assumed all the accusations and condemnations of the colonizer, that he is becoming accustomed to looking at his own people through the eyes of their procurer. True, they are not without defects, nor even without blame. There is concrete foundation for his impatience with them and their values. Almost everything in them is out of style, inefficient and derisory. But what is this? They are his own people, he is and has never ceased to be one of them at heart! Those rhythms balanced for centuries, that food which fills his mouth and stomach so well, they are still his own; they are still himself. Must he, all his life, be ashamed of what is most real in him, of the only things not borrowed? Must he insist on denying himself, and, moreover, will he always be able to stand it? Must his liberation be accomplished through systematic self-denial?

Nonetheless, the major impossibility is not negating one's existence, for he soon discovers that, even if he agrees to everything, he would not be saved. In order to be assimilated, it is not enough to leave one's group, but one must enter another; now he meets with the colonizer's rejection.

All that the colonized has done to emulate the colonizer has met with disdain from the colonial masters. They explain to the colonized that those efforts are in vain, that he only acquires thereby an additional trait, that of being ridiculous. He can never succeed in becoming identified with the colonizer, nor even in copying his role correctly. In the best of circumstances, if he does not want to offend the colonized too much, the colonizer will use all his psychological theories. The national character of peoples is incompatible; every gesture is subtended by the entire spirit, etc. If he is more rude, he will say that the colonized is an ape. The shrewder the ape, the better he imitates, and the more the colonizer becomes irritated. With that vigilance and a smell sharpened by malice, he will track down the telltale nuance in clothing or language, the "lack of good taste" which he always manages to discover. Indeed, a man straddling two cultures is rarely well seated, and the colonized does not always find the right pose.

Everything is mobilized so that the colonized cannot cross the doorstep, so that he understands and admits that this path is dead and assimilation is impossible.

This makes the regrets of humanists in the mother country very hollow, just as their reproach directed to the colonized is unjust. How dare he refuse that wonderful synthesis in which he can only win? It is the colonized who is the first to desire assimilation, and it is the colonizer who refuses it to him.

Now that colonization is reaching its end, tardy expressions of good will are heard asking whether assimilation was not the great opportunity missed by colonizers and mother countries. "Ah, if we had only agreed to it! Can't you imagine!" they daydream. "A France with one hundred million Frenchmen?" It is not forbidden to re-imagine history, and it is often consoling, but only on the condition that you discover another meaning to it, another hidden rationale.

Could assimilation have succeeded? Perhaps it could have at other periods of history. Under the conditions of contemporary colonization, apparently not. It may be a historical misfortune, and perhaps we should all deplore it together. Not only did it fail, but it appeared impossible to all parties concerned.

In the final analysis, its failure is due not only to the colonizer's bias but also to the colonized's backwardness. Assimilation, whether carried out or not, is not a question of good will or psychology alone. A sufficiently long series of happy circumstances can change the fate of an individual. A few of the colonized almost succeeded in disappearing into the colonizer group. It is clear, on the other hand, that a collective drama will never be settled through individual solutions. The individual disappears in his lineage and the group drama goes on. In order for assimilation of the colonized to have both purpose and meaning, it would have to affect an entire people; i.e., that the whole colonial condition be changed. However, the colonial condition cannot be changed except by doing away with the colonial relationship.

We again meet with the fundamental relationship which, dynamically meshed one with another, unites our two portraits. We see once again that it is useless to hope to act upon one or the other without affecting that relationship, and therefore, colonization. To say that the colonizer could or should accept assimilation and, hence, the colonized's emancipation, means to topple the colonial relationship. If not, it implies that he can proceed by himself to a complete overthrow of his status by condemning colonial privileges and the exorbitant rights of colonists and industrialists—paying colonized labor fairly, assuring juridical, administrative and political promotion of the colonized, industrializing the colony, etc. In other words, the end of the colony as a colony, and the end of the mother country as a mother country. To put it bluntly, the colonizer would be asked to put an end to himself.

Under the contemporary conditions of colonization, assimilation and colonization are contradictory.

What is there left then for the colonized to do? Being unable to change his condition in harmony and communion with the colonizer, he tries to become free despite him . . . he will revolt.

Far from being surprised at the revolts of colonized peoples, we should be, on the contrary, surprised that they are not more frequent and more violent. Actually, the colonizer guards against them in many ways: by continuous incapacitation of the leaders and periodic destruction of those who, despite everything, manage to come forward; by corruption or police oppression, aborting all popular movements and causing their brutal and rapid destruction. We have also noted the doubts of the colonized himself, the inadequacy of the aggressiveness of a vanquished who admires his conqueror despite himself, the long maintained hope that the almighty power of the colonizer might bear the fruit of infinite goodness.

However, revolt is the only way out of the colonial situation, and the colonized realizes it sooner or later. His condition is absolute and cries for an absolute solution; a break and not a compromise. He has been torn away from his past and cut off from his future, his traditions are dying and he loses the hope of acquiring a new culture. He has neither language, nor flag, nor technical knowledge, nor national or international existence, nor rights, nor duties. He possesses nothing, is no longer anything and no longer hopes for anything. Moreover, the solution becomes more urgent every day. The mechanism for destroying the colonized cannot but worsen daily. The more oppression increases, the more the colonizer needs justification. The more he must debase the colonized, the more guilty he feels, the more he must justify himself, etc. How can he emerge from this increasingly explosive circle except by rupture, explosion? The colonial situation, by its own internal inevitability, brings on revolt. For the colonial condition cannot be adjusted to; like an iron collar, it can only be broken.

We then witness a reversal of terms. Assimilation being abandoned, the colonized's liberation must be carried out through a recovery of self and of autonomous dignity. Attempts at imitating the colonizer required self-denial; the colonizer's rejection is the indispensable prelude to self-discovery. That accusing and annihilating image must be shaken off; oppression must be attacked boldly since it is impossible to go around it. After having been rejected for so long by the colonizer, the day has come when it is the colonized who must refuse the colonizer.

There can be no unconditional desire for assimilation if there is to follow a complete rejection of the model. At the height of his revolt, the colonized still bears the traces and lessons of prolonged cohabitation (just as the smile or movements of a wife, even during divorce proceedings, remind one strangely of those of her husband). The colonized fights in the name of the very values of the colonizer, uses his techniques of thought and his methods of combat. It must be added that this is the only action that the colonizer understands.

Henceforth, the colonizer adopts a negative approach. In particular, he is negatively induced by the active attitude of the colonized. He is challenged at every moment with respect to both his culture and his life, including his motherland. He is suspected, challenged and opposed in the least significant actions. With fury and ostentation, the colonized begins to show a preference for German cars, Italian radios and American refrigerators. He does without tobacco if it bears the colonialist's stamp! These are pressure methods and economic sanctions, but they are, equally, sacrificial rites of colonization. They continue until the terrible days of the colonizer's fury or the colonized's exasperation, which in turn culminate in hatred and explode into a bloody revolt. Then day-by-day living begins again, but a little more dramatically, more irremediably . . . more contradictory.

It is in this context that the colonized's xenophobia

and even a certain racism, must make their return.

Considered *en bloc* as *them, they* or *those*, different from every point of view, homogeneous in a radical heterogeneity, the colonized reacts by rejecting all the colonizers *en bloc*. The distinction between deed and intent has no great significance in the colonial situation. In the eyes of the colonized, all Europeans in the colonies are *de facto* colonizers, and whether they want to be or not, they are colonizers in some ways. By their privileged economic position, by belonging to the political system of oppression, or by participating in an effectively negative complex toward the colonized, they are colonizers. Furthermore, Europeans of Europe are potentially colonizers. All they need do is set foot on the colonized's land. Perhaps they even receive some benefit from colonization. They are supporters or at least unconscious accomplices of that great collective aggression of Europe. By their whole weight, intentionally or not, they contribute to the perpetuation of colonial oppression. If xenophobia and racism consist of accusing an entire human group as a whole, condemning each individual of that group, seeing in him an irremediably noxious nature, then the colonized has, indeed, become a xenophobe and a racist.

All racism and all xenophobia consist of delusions about oneself, including absurd and unjust aggressions toward others. Included are those of the colonized—the more so when they extend beyond the colonizers to everything which is not strictly colonized. When, for example, they are carried away by enjoyment of the misfortunes of another human group simply because it is not in slavery, they are guilty of xenophobia. However, it must be noted at the same time that the colonized's racism is the result of a more general delusion: the colonialist delusion.

Being considered and treated apart by colonialist racism, the colonized ends up accepting this Manichaean division of the colony and, by extension, of the whole world. Being definitely excluded from half the world, why should he not suspect it of confirming his condemnation? Why should he not judge it and condemn it in his turn? The racism of the colonized is then neither biological nor metaphysical, but social and historical. It is not based on a belief in the inferiority of the detested group but on the conviction, and in large measure on the observation, that this group is truly an aggressor and dangerous. Furthermore, while modern European racism hates and scorns more than it fears, that of the colonized fears and also continues to admire. In brief, it is not aggressive but defensive racism.

Thus, it should be relatively easy to appease. The few European voices raised during these past few years to repudiate this exclusion and inhumanity of the colonized, did more than all the good works and philanthropy in which segregation remained subjacent. That is why one can say that though the xenophobia and racism of the colonized undoubtedly contain enormous resentment and are a negative force, they could be the prelude to a positive movement, the regaining of self-control by the colonized.

However, at the beginning, the colonized's claim is narrowly limited and conditioned by the colonial situation and the requirements of the colonizer.

The colonized accepts and asserts himself with passion. But who is he? Surely not man in general, the holder of universal values common to all men. In fact, he has been excluded from that universality, both in word and in fact. On the contrary, what makes him different from other men has been sought out and hardened to the point of substantiation. He has been haughtily shown that he could never assimilate with others; he has been scornfully thrown back toward what is in him which could not be assimilated by others. Very well, then! He is, he shall be, that man. The same passion which made him admire and absorb Europe shall make him assert his differences; since those differences, after all, are within him and correctly constitute his true self.

Now, the young intellectual who had broken with religions, internally at least, and ate during Ramadan, begins to fast with ostentation. He who considered the rites as inevitable family drudgery, reintroduces them into his social life, gives them a place in his conception of the world. To use them better, he re-explains the forgotten messages and adapts them to present-day needs. He then discovers that religion is not simply an attempt to communicate with the invisible, but also an extraordinary place of communion for the whole group. The colonized, his leaders and intellectuals, his traditionalists and liberals, all classes of society, can meet there, reinforce their bonds, verify and re-create their unity. Of course, there is a considerable risk that the means become the end. Assigning attention to the old myths, giving them virility, he regenerates them dangerously. They find in this an unexpected power which makes them extend beyond the limited intentions of the colonized's leaders. We see a true return to religion. It may even happen that the sorcerer's apprentice, intellectual or liberal bourgeois, to whom secularization appeared to be the condition for all intellectual and social progress, might be attracted to those neglected traditions, that his pressured mind. . . .

However, all that, which seems so important in the eyes of an outside observer, and which is so perhaps for the general welfare of the people, is basically secondary to the colonized. He has now discovered the motivating principle of his battle. He must bolster his people and affirm his own solidarity with it. Obviously, his religion is one of the constituent elements of that people. At Bandung, to the astonishment and embarrassment of leftists all over the world, one of the two fundamental principles of the conference was religion.

Likewise, the colonized no longer knew his language except in the form of a lowly dialect. In order to emerge from the most elementary monotony and emotions, he had to borrow the colonizer's language. In recovering his autonomous and separate destiny, he immediately goes back to his own tongue. It is pointed out to him that its vocabulary is limited, its syntax bastardized. It would be comical to hear a course in higher mathematics or philosophy in it. Even the left-wing colonizer is surprised by this unnecessary challenge which is more costly in the long run to the colonized than to the colonizer. Why not go on using Western languages to describe motors or teach abstract subjects?

Again, there exist other urgent matters for the colonized besides mathematics and philosophy and even technology. To this self-rediscovery movement of an entire people must be returned the most appropriate tool; that which finds the shortest path to its soul, because it comes directly from it. That path is words of love and tenderness, anger and indignation, words which the potter uses when talking to his pots, and the shoemaker to his soles. Education will come later, and so will the humanities and sciences. These people have learned all too well how to wait. Besides, is it certain that this language which stammers today is unable to develop and become rich? Thanks to him, it is already discovering forgotten treasures. It is beginning to see a possible continuity with a past which is not inconsequential. No more hesitation and half-measures! On the contrary, one must know how to break through, one must know how to forge ahead. He will even choose the greatest of all difficulties. He will go so far as to prohibit any additional conveniences of the colonizer's tongue; he will replace it as often and as soon as he can. Between the vulgar tongue and scholarly language, he will give preference to the scholarly, running the risk of making the sought-after communion more arduous. The important thing now is to rebuild his people, whatever be their authentic nature; to reform their unity, communicate with it and to feel that they belong.

This must be done no matter what the price paid by the colonized. Thus he will be nationalistic but not, of course, internationalistic. Naturally, by so doing, he runs the risk of falling into exclusionism and chauvinism, of sticking to the most narrow principles, and of setting national solidarity against human solidarity—and even ethnic solidarity against national solidarity. But to expect the colonized to open his mind to the world and be a humanist and internationalist would seem to be ludicrous thoughtlessness. He is still regaining possession of himself, still examining himself with astonishment, passionately demanding the return of his language.

Moreover, it is remarkable that he is even more ardent in asserting himself as he tries to assume the identity of the colonizer. Is it a coincidence that so many colonized leaders contracted mixed marriages? That the Tunisian leader Bourguiba, the two Algerian leaders Messali Hadj and Ferhat Abbas, that several other nationalists who have devoted their lives to leading their own people, chose a wife from among the colonizers? Having penetrated the colonizer's experience to the highest limit, to the point of finding it unlivable, they withdrew to their own bases. Whoever has not left his country and his people will never understand to what extent those are dear to him. Now they know that their salvation coincides with that of their people and that they must cling as closely as possible to them and to their traditions.

The necessity of self-renewal is as obvious as the ambiguity involved. While the colonized's revolt is a clear attitude in itself, its contents may be muddled; for it is the result of an unclear situation—the colonial situation.

First, by taking up the challenge of exclusion, the colonized accepts being separate and different, but his individuality is that which is limited and defined by the colonizer.

Thus he embodies religion and tradition, ineptitude for technology of a special nature which we call Eastern, etc. Yes, that is quite right, he agrees with it. A black author did his best to explain to us that the nature of the blacks, his own people, is not compatible with mechanized civilization. He drew a curious pride from that. So then, no doubt provisionally, the colonized admits that he corresponds to that picture of himself which the colonizer has thrust upon him. He is starting a new life but continues to subscribe to the colonizers' deception.

To be sure, he does not arrive at it by a purely ideological process; he is not only defined by the colonizer, but his situation is shaped by colonization. It is obvious that he is reclaiming a people that is suffering deficiencies in its body and spirit, in its responses. He is restored to a not very glorious history pierced through with frightful holes, to a moribund culture which he had planned to abandon, to frozen traditions, to a rusted tongue. The heritage which he eventually accepts bears the burden of a liability which would discourage anyone. He must endorse notes and debts, the debts being many and large. It is also a fact that the institutions of the colony do not operate directly for him. The educational system is directed to him only haphazardly. The roads are open to him only because they are pure offerings.

But to go all the way with his revolt, it seems necessary to him to accept those inhibitions and amputations. He will forego the use of the colonizer's language, even if all the locks of the country turn with that key; he will change the signs and highway markings, even if he is the first to be inconvenienced. He will prefer a long period of educational mistakes to the continuance of the colonizer's school organization. He will choose institutional disorder in order to destroy the institutions built by the colonizer as soon as possible. There we see, indeed, a reactive drive of profound protest. He will no longer owe anything to the colonizer and will have definitely broken with him. But this also involves a confused and misleading conviction: everything that belongs to the colonizer is not appropriate for the colonized. That is just what the colonizer always told him. Briefly, the rebellious colonized begins by accepting himself as something negative.

A second point is that the negative element has become an essential part of his revival and struggle, and will be proclaimed and glorified to the hilt. Not only does he accept his wrinkles and his wounds, but he will consider them praiseworthy. Gaining self-assurance, offering himself to the world just as he is, he can hardly propose criticism of himself at the same time. While he knows how to overthrow the colonizer and colonization, he cannot cause the end of what he truly is and what he so disastrously acquired during colonization. He offers himself as a whole and agrees that he is what he is—that colonized being which he has become. Suddenly, exactly to the reverse of the colonialist accusation, the colonized, his culture, his country, everything that belongs to him, everything he represents, become perfectly positive elements.

We shall ultimately find ourselves before a countermythology. The negative myth thrust on him by the colonizer is succeeded by a positive myth about himself suggested by the colonized—just as there would seem to be a positive myth of the proletarian opposed to a negative one. To hear the colonized and often his friends, everything is good, everything must be retained among his customs and traditions, his actions and plans; even the anachronous or disorderly, the immoral or mistaken. Everything is justified because everything can be explained.

The colonized's self-assertion, born out of a protest, continues to define itself in relation to it. In the midst of revolt, the colonized continues to think, feel and live against and, therefore, in relation to the colonizer and colonization.

It must also be said that the colonized has a presentiment of all this, revealing it in his conduct, and even admitting it at times. Realizing that these attitudes are essentially reactions, he suffers from the pangs of bad faith.

Uncertain of himself, he gives in to the intoxication of fury and violence. In fact, he asserts himself vigorously. Uncertain of being able to convince others, he provokes them. Simultaneously provocative and sensitive, he now makes a display of his contrasts, refuses to let himself be forgotten as such, and becomes indignant when they are mentioned. Automatically distrustful, he assumes hostile intentions in those with whom he converses and reacts accordingly. He demands endless approval from his best friends, of even that which he doubts and himself condemns. Frustrated by history for too long, he makes demands all the more imperiously as he continues to be restless. He no longer knows what he owes to himself and what he can ask, what others actually owe him and what he must pay in return. He complicates and confuses, *a priori*, his human relationships, which history has already made so difficult. "Oh, they are sick!" wrote another black author. "They are all sick!"

So goes the drama of the man who is a product and victim of colonization. He almost never succeeds in corresponding with himself.

Colonized painting, for instance, is balanced between two poles. From excessive submission to Europe resulting in depersonalization, it passes to such a violent return to self that it is noxious and esthetically illusory. The right balance not being found, the self-accusation continues. Before and during the revolt, the colonized always considers the colonizer as a model or as an antithesis. He continues to struggle against him. He was torn between what he was and what he wanted to be, and now he is torn between what he wanted to be and what he is making of himself. Nonetheless, the painful discord with himself continues.

In order to witness the colonized's complete cure, his alienation must completely cease. We must await the complete disappearance of colonization—including the period of revolt.

PART THREE

CONCLUSION

Conclusion

I know very well that after this diagnosis the reader now expects remedies. I did not conceive of this book as a work of protest or even as a search for solutions. It was born out of reflection on an accepted failure.

For many of us who rejected the face of Europe in the colony, there was no question of rejecting Europe in its entirety. We only wanted it to recognize our rights, just as we were prepared to assume our duties. We wanted a simple arrangement of our relations with Europe. To our surprise and sorrow, we slowly realized that such a hope was in vain, and I wanted to understand and explain why. My plan was only to reproduce, completely and authentically, the portraits of the two protagonists of the colonial drama and the relationship which binds them.

No one had ever shown the pattern and genesis of each role, the genesis of one through the other and the pattern of the colonial relationship, the genesis of the colonial relationship out of the colonial situation.

I realized the necessity of this relationship, the necessity of its development, the necessary images which it impressed on the colonizer and the colonized. Finally, a complete and careful analysis of those two portraits and that situation led me to con-

clude that the arrangement could not take place because it was impossible. Contemporary colonization
carried an inherent contradiction which, sooner or
later, would cause it to die.

Understand that there is no question here of a wish
but of an affidavit. Confusion of these two ideas
seems to me to be all too frequent and injurious now-
adays. It nevertheless radically separates all serious
and objective thought from sentimental projections
or demagogic deceits on which politicians too frequently rely (without too well realizing it, let us say
in their defense). There is no immutability in politics,
and a situation can often be rectified. But the desire
to effect a change must not go beyond the boundaries
of objective facts. What is apparent at the end of this
path—if the two portraits are accurate—is that it is
impossible for the colonial situation to last because
it is impossible to arrange it properly.

All analysis is, in the end, effective. All truth is
useful and positive because it cuts through illusion.
When one thinks of the desperate efforts of Europe
to save colonization, so costly for her as well as for
the colonized, this truth becomes obvious.

It must be added, nevertheless, that the disclosures
having been made, the cruelty of the truth having
been admitted, the relationship of Europe with her
former colonies must be reconsidered. Having
abandoned the colonial framework, it is important
for all of us to discover a new way of living with

that relationship. I am one of those who believe that to find a new order of things with Europe means putting new order in oneself.

So much said, I continue to hope that the reader distinguishes this human balance sheet of colonization from the lessons which I believe it is possible to draw from it. I know that I shall often have to ask that I be read before being refuted. I hope for an additional effort; and that, if opposed *a priori* to the lessons of this investigation, the reader does not reject that methodological but healthy prudence. We shall see later whether it is proper to acknowledge the necessity of the following conclusions.

It definitely appears that the colonizer is a disease of the European, from which he must be completely cured and protected. There is also a drama of the colonizer which would be absurd and unjust to underestimate. The cure involves difficult and painful treatment, extraction and reshaping of present conditions of existence. Nonetheless, there is also a drama, a still more serious one, if colonization continues.

Colonization can only disfigure the colonizer. It places him before an alternative having equally disastrous results; daily injustice accepted for his benefit on the one hand and necessary, but never consummated, self-sacrifice on the other. That is the situation with the colonizer who individually decays if he accepts, and repudiates himself if he refuses to accept.

The leftist colonizer's role cannot long be sustained; it is unlivable. He cannot help suffering from guilt and anguish and also, eventually, bad faith. He is always on the fringe of temptation and shame, and in the final analysis, guilty. The analysis of the colonial situation by the colonialist is more coherent and perhaps more lucid, for he has always acted as though an arrangement were impossible. Having realized that any concession threatened him, he confirms and defends the colonial system in every way. But what privileges, what material advantages, are worth the loss of his soul? In short, if the colonial adventure is seriously damaging for the colonized, it cannot but be unprofitable for the colonizer.

Naturally, people did not fail to devise changes that would leave the colonizer all the advantages acquired while sparing him the disastrous consequences. They only forget that the nature of the colonial relationship depends on its advantages. Either the colonial situation subsists and it effects nothing, or it disappears and the colonial relationship and colonizer disappear. The same goes for two propositions, one of them believed radical in a bad sense, the other believed radical in a good sense: extermination of the colonized or assimilation.

It has not been so long since Europe abandoned the idea of a possible total extermination of a colonized group. It has been said, half-seriously, with respect to Algeria: "There are only nine Algerians for each Frenchman. All that would be necessary would be to give each Frenchman a gun and nine bullets." The American example is also evoked; and it is undeniable that the famous national epic of the Far West greatly resembles systematic massacre. In any case, there is no longer much of an Indian problem in the United States. (Extermination saves colonization so little that it actually contradicts the colonial process.) Colonization is, above all, economic and political exploitation. If the colonized is eliminated, the colony becomes a country like any other, and who then will be exploited? Along with the colonized, colonization would disappear, and so would the colonizer.

As for the failure of assimilation, I do not derive any particular joy from it, especially since that solution carries a universalistic and socialistic flavor which makes it *a priori* respectable. I will not even say that it is impossible by definition; historically, it has succeeded a few times, but it has often failed. However, it is clear that no one expressly desired assimilation in contemporary colonization, not even the Communists. Moreover, and this is the essential thing, assimilation is also the opposite of colonization. It tends to eliminate the distinctions between the colonizers and the colonized, and thereby eliminates the colonial relationship.

I shall pass over minor pseudosolutions: for example, to remain as foreigners in a colony that has become independent; thereby having no special rights. It is obvious that, besides the legal incongruity of such proposals, such an arrangement is destined to be worn down by history. One can scarcely see why the memory of unjust privileges would be sufficient to guarantee their permanence. In any case, there is apparently no hope for the colonizer within the framework of colonization.

Some will say that this is one more reason for him to hang on, to refuse any change. He can then accept being a monster, accept alienation through his own interests. But no, not even that. If he refuses to abandon his profitable sicknesses, he will sooner or later be forced to do so by history. For let us not forget, the diptych has another side: one day he will be forced by the colonized to give in.

A day necessarily comes when the colonized lifts his head and topples the always unstable equilibrium of colonization. For the colonized just as for the colonizer, there is no way out other than a complete end to colonization. The refusal of the colonized cannot be anything but absolute, that is, not only revolt, but a revolution.

Revolt. The mere existence of the colonizer creates

oppression, and only the complete liquidation of colonization permits the colonized to be freed. Much has been expected of reforms in recent times, of *bourguibisme,* for example. It seems to me that there is a misunderstanding. *Bourguibisme,* if it means to proceed by stages, never meant being satisfied with any stage, whatever it might be. The leaders of the blacks presently speak of a French Union. Again, it is only one stage on the road to complete and inevitable independence. If Bourguiba should believe in the *bourguibisme* ascribed to him, and the leaders of Black Africa believe in a permanent French Union, the process of liquidating colonization would leave them behind. Already, the younger generation fails to understand the relative moderation of their elders.

Revolution. We have seen that colonization materially kills the colonized. It must be added that it kills him spiritually. Colonization distorts relationships, destroys or petrifies institutions, and corrupts men, both colonizers and colonized. To live, the colonized needs to do away with colonization. To become a man, he must do away with the colonized being that he has become. If the European must annihilate the colonizer within himself, the colonized must rise above his colonized being.

The liquidation of colonization is nothing but a prelude to complete liberation, to self-recovery. In order to free himself from colonization, the colonized must start with his oppression, the deficiencies of his group. In order that his liberation may be complete, he must free himself from those inevitable conditions of his struggle. A nationalist, because he had to fight for the emergence and dignity of his nation, he must conquer himself and be free in relation to that nation. He can, of course, assert himself as a nationalist. But it is indispensable that he have a free choice and not that he exist only through his nation. He must conquer himself and be free in relation to the religion of his group, which he can retain or reject, but he must stop existing only through it. The same applies to the past, tradition, ethnic characteristics, etc. Finally, he must cease defining himself through the categories of colonizers. The same holds true of what more subtly characterizes him in a negative way. For example, the famous and absurd incompatibility between East and West, that antithesis hardened by the colonizer, who thereby sets up a permanent barrier between himself and the colonized. What does the return to the East mean, anyway? Even if oppression has assumed the face of England or France, cultural and technical acquirements belong to all peoples. Science is neither Western nor Eastern, any more than it is bourgeois or proletarian. There are only two ways of pouring concrete—the right way and the wrong way.

What will he then become? What is the colonized, in actual fact? I believe neither in metaphysical essence nor in psychological essence. One can describe the colonized at present. I have tried to show that he suffers, judges and behaves in a certain manner. If he ceases to be a colonized—he will become something else. Geography and tradition are obviously permanent forces. But perhaps at that time there will be fewer differences between an Algerian and a Marseillais than between an Algerian and a Lebanese.

Having reconquered all his dimensions, the former colonized will have become a man like any other. There will be the ups and downs of all men to be sure, but at least he will be a whole and free man.

Afterword

Nineteen fifty-six was a pivotal year in the history of the decolonization of French North Africa. In March of that year, the former protectorates of Tunisia and Morocco achieved a settlement with France and began to breathe the air of freedom. In neighboring Algeria, a bloody insurrection led by Muslim nationalists reached a crescendo of brutality that shocked the conscience of the world. Northern Africa was in a ferment of revolution, and the speed of cataclysmic change was disorienting participant and onlooker alike. The trappings of French imperial rule, painstakingly assembled over the previous century, were coming apart at the seams, and no one quite understood why. This was the moment when Albert Memmi took on the task of explaining to the world the personalities, the processes, and the inevitable outcomes of the colonialist condition; the result was *The Colonizer and the Colonized*, first published in Paris in 1957.

In Memmi's words, his purpose was to "reproduce, completely and authentically, the portraits of the

Quotations in this afterword are Memmi's own words, taken from *La Statue de Sel*, Paris, 1966 (English translation, *The Pillar of Salt*, New York, 1955); *La terre intérieure: Entretiens avec Victor Malka*, Paris, 1976; and a conversation I had with Albert Memmi in Paris in June 1990.

two protagonists in the colonial drama and the relationship that binds them." The title of the essay
in French, *Le Portrait du Colonisé précédé d'un Portrait
du Colonisateur*, captures two key ideas in the conception of the work: first, the notion of the "portrait"
of the main actors as two actual personality types,
rather than as vague abstractions unanchored in reality; and second, the idea that these two types, created by necessity to sustain the colonialist condition,
are tied together in a "duo" of mutual need. Memmi
described with striking imagery how the existence
of one was bound up with the other, and how their
relationship had a fatality that could be broken only
by radical change.

Memmi was uniquely positioned to give a faithful
rendering of the colonialist dilemma, for he spoke
from a position of deep immersion in the politics of
oppression. He was, after all, a Tunisian, and a Jew
at that, therefore a member of a subset of the sub-
missive. But along with the depth of understanding
that came from having lived the experience of the
colonized, he wrote in eloquent French and had the
gift of powerful expression in the language of the
colonizer. Together, these two qualities combined
to construct a persuasive argument.

In his essay, Memmi begins by telling his friends
on the French Left, former members of the Resistance such as Sartre and Camus, that the empire is

doomed; there is no conceivable compromise that will allow the foreigner to stay. Moreover, there are no "moral" or "immoral" Europeans in the colonies, he says, there are only colonizers, forced to exploit in order to enjoy the fruits of colonialism—wealth, prestige, and easy living. At bottom, all colonizers, even those with the best of intentions, are "usurpers," miniature Neros driven beyond reason to take what is not theirs. Likewise, there are no colonized worthy of being called "men," for beneath a veneer of calm normalcy, they too are disfigured by the disease of servitude.

This pessimistic reading of the colonialist situation contains within it a logical solution, even though many, both in the colonies and the home country, were not ready to pay heed. Inundating his reader with examples shot through with the echoes of painful personal experience, Memmi drives home his message: the only cure for the pathological condition that colonization inflicts on colonizer and colonized alike is national liberation. "The colonial condition cannot be adjusted to; like an iron collar, it can only be broken." He concludes with the prophetic warning that freedom for the colonized and a return home for the colonizer is the only release from the prison of colonialism.

Like the writings of Franz Fanon, the Madagascan psychiatrist and author who was the voice of the

Algerian revolution, Memmi's analysis in *The Colonizer and the Colonized* was seized upon by leaders of a generation in revolt as a blueprint for action. When the book first appeared, the leftist *L'Observateur* called it "the most disturbing . . . of the year," and according to Memmi, it was frequently found by colonial police in the cells of militants. The French text almost immediately went through three separate editions (1957, 1966, 1973) and was published in Quebec in 1972. It was also translated into Japanese (1959), into English for two American editions (1965, 1967), into Portuguese (1967, 1974), into Spanish (1969, 1971), into Basque (1974), and into Italian (1979).

While the furor of the early years of decolonization has long since passed, along with the specific historical conditions under which *The Colonizer and the Colonized* was written, the importance of the book has not diminished over time. Would-be revolutionaries may no longer conceal it in prison cells, but the work is still sought after by students of nationalism, imperialism, and racism as a lucid exposition of the theoretical underpinnings of the colonialist condition, filtered through the prism of lived experience. Memmi's thoughts regarding dependence, racial oppression, and the dynamics of social conflict have been borne out by subsequent social science research, while the raw vividness of his own testi-

mony permeates the work, as Sartre says, "with
human intentions and felt relationships."

Albert Memmi was born in Tunis on December
15, 1920, "two steps from" the Hara, or old Jewish
quarter, where the majority of the Jews of Tunis
lived crowded together in tumble-down, "shapeless"
houses separated by teeming alleyways. Although
his father was a craftsman, a saddlemaker who owned
his own shop, the family lived on the margins of
poverty. Memmi tells in *The Pillar of Salt* (*La Statue
de Sel*), an autobiographical work barely disguised
as fiction, how as a young boy he realized with
sudden shame that most of his clothes were second-
hand. The humiliation of being poor weighed on
his childhood and later embittered his feelings toward the propertied classes.

His father was of Italian Jewish origins, his mother
from "native" Jewish Berber stock. Neither was
well educated; his father had some schooling, but
his mother was illiterate and spoke only the Judeo-
Arabic of the Hara, a mélange of Arabic, Hebrew,
and Mediterranean loan-words that made up the
lingua franca of the Jews of Tunis. At the age of
four Memmi was sent to a nearby Talmudic school,
where he learned to read Hebrew and recite the
prayers; when he reached seven, he entered the primary school of the Alliance Israélite Universelle.

The French-sponsored AIU schools in Tunis and throughout the Middle East offered to Jewish children of humble origins a Western secular education, at a time when most government-run schools were reserved for the offspring of the colonial elite.

At the AIU school, Memmı suddenly had to speak French. He describes the experience as follows: "I faced an abyss, without any means of communicating with the far side. The instructor spoke only French and I spoke only the dialect: how would we ever be able to meet?" His situation was hardly unique; countless other children of the colonies found themselves in a similar predicament, forced to leave behind their "basic unity" and to seek a new identity in the territory of the other, of "re-assembling . . . their scattered limbs." Memmi's struggle with French consumed his growing years. To speak as his bourgeois friends did, to wear with ease the mantle of *la civilisation française* which was the patrimony of every schoolchild, French or otherwise, who passed through the French colonial school system, became his burning ambition.

Memmi was a brilliant student and at the age of twelve won a scholarship from the Jewish community of Tunis to attend the Lycée Carnot, the French-run high school that was a principal training ground for the Tunisian political elite. Normally, a high school education was a luxury that only the sons of the middle and upper classes could afford. It meant not only high tuition fees but also lost wages, for most boys of the *ouvrier* class usually joined their fathers as apprentices as soon as they reached working age. On entering the *lycée*, Memmi crossed the threshold from the society of the colonized to that of the colonizer. The transition made him acutely aware of his multiple identities and the contradictions among them. His very name was a signifier of the two main poles that drew him: the Albert of the "wonderful West" and the African-sounding Memmi, whom he imagined as "a family of Berber princes converted to Judaism by Kahena, the [Jewish] warrior-queen of the Atlas Mountains." Torn by opposing selves, he consciously willed for himself a new *persona* enfolding several identities, each of them subjugated: "I'm . . . a native in a colonial country," he announced, "a Jew in an anti-Semitic universe, an African in a world dominated by Europe."

Also at the *lycée*, Memmi awoke to the experience of exclusion from the society of the elite, a sensation which deeply frustrated him and finally motivated him to write. During these years he developed his lifelong stance as the perpetual outsider, shut out by birth and inclination from the circles of the elect, yet watching them and scrupulously reporting on their behavior. Distancing himself from his own origins, he drew no closer to belonging to the other. In *The Pillar of Salt*, Memmi describes with clinical detachment his agonizing separation from his Jewish roots, his deliberate rejection of the rituals of the "tribe," his anger and resentment toward his bourgeois schoolmates: "I saw clearly that cutting myself off entirely from my own original background did not necessarily allow me to enter any other group. Just as I sat on the fence between two civilizations, so would I now find myself between two classes . . . ." Jewish, Tunisian, and poor, Memmi adopted a new personality, that of the "alien, a critical and bad-tempered stranger, a spectator that watched from the side."

Thus positioning himself, he saw things afresh and differently from others, and this insight, coupled with his supple use of the French language, formed the sources for his literary creativity. Not long after finishing the *lycée*, Memmi began writing for several Tunisian newspapers. His first important effort, a series on Jewish literature, appeared in *Le Petit Matin* in 1942. Soon after, he went to Algiers where he began university studies in philosophy, but the war intervened, and he went home to Nazi-occupied Tunis, where he was almost immediately interred in a German work camp. The terrifying story of his escape and return home is told in *The Pillar of Salt*. When the war ended, he left for France and graduate studies in philosophy at the Sorbonne, where he met his future wife, the "blond and blue-eyed Marie." His "mixed marriage" with her became the metaphor for his struggle to reconcile the two halves of his soul, the European and the African. Still seeking his proper place, he returned to Tunis in 1951 to teach and was soon embroiled in the nationalist struggle, which he fully supported. But the nationalist victory brought him no peace, and by 1956 he had left Tunisia for permanent exile in France. That same year he wrote *The Colonizer and the Colonized* (his second book after the autobiographical *The Pillar of Salt*, which was published in 1953).

The notoriety of the new book launched a literary career that now embraces half a dozen major works of fiction, an equal number of book-length essays, short stories, poetry, plays, introductions to editions, contributions to collections, interviews, lectures, book reviews, and countless newspaper and journal articles. Today, at the age of seventy, Albert Memmi's writing appears regularly in France, still characterized by an intimate relationship between his life and his art, still animated by his singular ability to make collective responses comprehensible through an analysis of individual interactions.

The Colonizer and the Colonized is in many respects a product of its time. While the dynamics of the relationship between master and servant, oppressor and oppressed, have a universality that transcends time and place, in some matters Memmi's views have been superseded by more recent thinking that makes his own seem dated. Memmi's view of women, for example, reflects a male-centered stance that the author himself has come to regret. In this work colonizer and colonized are always men, both implicitly and explicitly: "Having conquered all his dimensions, the former colonized will *become a man* (italics are mine) like any other. . . ." No women are mentioned among those longing to be free, although women played an active role in all of the North African revolutionary movements, and particularly in the bloody battle of Algiers. Memmi is impartial in his omission, for women do not appear among the ranks of the colonizers either, although colonial wives would often exercise a vicious and petty tyranny over their domestic servants. Good or evil, women as personalities in the colonialist drama are largely absent from Memmi's account.

Yet we know that women were agents on both sides in the process of colonization and decolonization, just as we know that the ultimate expression of authority on the part of colonizers, and of liberation on the part of the colonized, was the sexual possession of the women of the other. Hence the powerful undertones of the "mixed marriage," which for Memmi may have been a genuine effort at "reconciliation," but for other ex-servants, became a means of asserting male dominance over the most cherished possession of the former master. There is no need to delve deeply into the psychology of oppression to understand that the politics of alien rule induced its own sexual responses.

Another subject in which the work reflects the intellectual climate of its day is the issue of language. For Memmi and others of his generation, mastery of French was the great challenge, the obstacle between themselves and acceptance in the world of the European. In *The Pillar of Salt*, Memmi tells of his struggle to roll his *r*'s properly and to choose the correct turn of phrase so that his spoken language would be indistinguishable from that of his French classmates. At the same time, he assumed that the primacy of French meant a downgrading of the dialect, which for him was the language of "love and tenderness, anger and indignation." The demotion of the mother tongue to second place was a "cultural catastrophe . . . never completely overcome."

But today, unlike the time of Memmi's youth, we see peoples who were once colonized now fully at ease in multiple languages, their own and the languages of their former colonizers. Mastering the language of the other is no longer seen as cause for a "cultural crisis"; rather, it is regarded as a natural and necessary step for those who aspire to lead in their society. It is true that the tool of bilingualism still tends to be the preserve of the political and social elite, often restricted by the politics of scarcity to the wealthy and the few. But as Benedict Anderson has pointed out in his book on nationalism, *Imag-*

ined Communities, "it is a mistake to treat languages . . . as *emblems* of nation-ness . . . [for] the important thing about language is its capacity for generating . . . solidarities." Whether members of the community speak French, Arabic, or both is immaterial so long as the language in use is a vehicle for nation-building. The variety of strategies available to political leaders today to conjure up a sense of solidarity—the press, television, music, and sports, for example—were simply unavailable in Memmi's time, when language stood out as one of the few symbols of national identity.

These points aside, Memmi's work has endured. His writing is often included in anthologies of North African literature in French, alongside figures such as Tahar Ben Jelloun, Kateb Yacine, Driss Chraibi, and others. Yet Memmi remains an anomaly, standing apart in self-imposed isolation. He tells us this is because of his Jewishness; yet his experience of oppression as a Jew is the one that made him sensitive to the condition of colonial servitude. Judaism for him was both a weighty burden and a source of inspiration: Memmi wrote as he did because he was a Jew and in spite of his being a Jew, for he found little comfort in his faith. In his outrage against the terms of the colonial encounter, Memmi responded to a profound sense of social justice that is closely akin to Jewish ethics and historical memory: "When I see an injustice taking place in the street, I suffer to the point of physical illness, to the point of panic. . . . It is a matter of identification with the victim. . . . I am unable to stand an injustice, I cannot live calmly in an unjust society." His complex attitudes toward his Jewishness, toward his Arabness (which he also acknowledges as an intimate part of his character), together with his liberal humanitarian impulses, set up subtle oppositions that place him far beyond the limits of the ordinary, in a unique space created by his own genius.

The present edition is a reprint of the earlier 1967 English edition, which was in turn a reissue of the original 1965 English edition. The translation by Howard Greenfeld is a graceful rendering of the original; Memmi's dedication to "the American Negro" links his work to the civil rights movement in the United States, then at flood tide.

The introduction by Jean-Paul Sartre is also intellectually and historically significant; it appears here as it did in the first French edition of 1957. Memmi and Sartre were friends, although Memmi did not share Sartre's dedication to Marxist thought which was in vogue among the European left in the postwar years. Memmi found Marxism "too romantic, too irrational, and too *à la mode*" and was wary of those who held it beyond question. Because of his own healthy respect for the power of human emotions, Memmi was repulsed by the rigid determinism of some Marxist thinkers, just as he equally deplored the dogmatism of the reactionary right.

Although there was admiration, and even warmth, between Memmi and Sartre, there were sharp differences between them in the manner in which they viewed the colonialist condition. Sartre saw it as a "system," a natural outcome of the economic "apparatus" geared to exploit subject peoples. Colonialism, in his view, was good business, buying cheap and selling dear, while providing "the natives" little in the way of comfort or hope. Memmi agreed with this in theory, but he rejected it as a methodological approach. For him, colonialism was not a drama based on the impersonal operation of economic forces but rather a flesh and blood encounter between two protean elements, one driven by a lust for power, the other by a longing for justice. What for Sartre was textbook economics was for Memmi a passion play fraught with universal meanings.

Yet Sartre's argument has its own poignancy, for he speaks with the voice of the disappointed French liberal, nauseated by the actions of the French army in Algeria, with its tactics of torture, its brutish "rat-hunts" in which humans were the prey. His main concern is his fellow countrymen, who silently collaborate in colonial wars. Memmi, too, talks to this constituency, but it is Sartre, the cult figure of the French left, who drives home the point that colonial wars are undermining the fiber of the nation. Disgust is no absolution, he says, and silence compounds the crime. We must act existentially and take part in the revolt of the oppressed, because it heralds the final stage in the dismemberment of the capitalist system.

These thoughts, too, belong to another time, when those who survived the whirlwind of European war thought they could build a better, braver world on the ruins of the old. Sartre and Memmi shared the experience of growing to maturity in the age of empire, of surviving the fury of the war years, and of suddenly finding themselves on the other side, with all the old rules in disarray. Neither had lost faith in human goodness, and both wanted to create new forms of social organization that would allow for the rekindling of the human spirit. They saw in the end of colonialism the promise that a more rational moment was at hand, in which, as Memmi says, people would be "whole and free." Memmi's essay and Sartre's introduction to it are living texts that evoke with eternal freshness the hope that the end of colonialism brought to people of good will, rulers and ruled alike, in the immediate postwar era.

Susan Gilson Miller
Cambridge, Massachusetts
September 1990

Albert
Memmi

The author of *The Colonizer and the Colonized* was
born on December 15, 1920, in Tunis, where he spent
his entire youth. During World War II he was ar-
rested and interned in a forced labor camp from
which he managed to escape. After the war he
studied at the University of Algiers and at the Sorbonne in Paris, where he received his degree in
philosophy. Since that time he has taught both in
Tunis and in Paris, where he now lives with his wife
and three children.

Mr. Memmi's other books have included two novels,
The Pillar of Salt and *Strangers,* as well as *Portrait
of a Jew.*